13

D0254220

Merchant to Romania

BUSINESS AS MISSIONS IN
POST-COMMUNIST EASTERN EUROPE

BX
695
.L58
2009

CCU Library
8787 W. Alameda Ave.
Lakewood, CO 80226

© Day One Publications 2009
First printed 2009

ISBN 978–1–84625–171–9

British Library Cataloguing in Publication Data available

Unless otherwise indicated, Scripture quotations in this publication are from the **New International Version** (NIV), copyright ©1973, 1978, 1984, International Bible Society. Used by permission of Hodder and Stoughton, a member of the Hodder Headline Group. All rights reserved.

Published by Day One Publications
Ryelands Road, Leominster, HR6 8NZ
☎ 01568 613 740 FAX 01568 611 473
email—sales@dayone.co.uk
web site—www.dayone.co.uk
North American—e-mail—sales@dayonebookstore.com
North American—web site—www.dayonebookstore.com

All rights reserved
No part of this publication may be reproduced, or stored in a retrieval system, or transmitted, in any form or by any means, mechanical, electronic, photocopying, recording or otherwise, without the prior permission of Day One Publications.

Cover design by Kathryn Chedgzoy
Printed in the USA

My life has been touched, encouraged and heavily impacted by watching what God can do with a businessman truly sold out to Him. Jeri Little is clearly a modern-day Barnabas, who "sold a field he owned and brought the money and put it at the apostles' feet" (Acts 4:37). Jeri's vision has had powerful and lasting results as God has led him to use his business skills to create self-sustaining and profitable ventures to provide local funding for ministry, badly needed jobs for local villagers and a platform for the gospel. God's bottom line is changed lives for Christ, and God has used Jeri and Gloria to achieve amazing results for Him—countless changed lives. Oh, that I would be as sold out as Jeri Little!

Tracy Schmidt, CFO, CNL Financial Group, Orlando, Florida, and former CFO, FedEx

This book is much more than the narrative of the production of a viable business as mission in Romania. It's the story of the global, missional God wooing his people into sacrifice that becomes joy … The book is marked by honesty, mistakes made, and challenges faced in the creation of authentic partnerships in order to make a viable mission business work.

William D. Taylor, Ph.D., Global Ambassador, World Evangelical Alliance and the Mission Commission

From the moment I visited Jeri and Gloria in Romania, I knew this was a story that had to be told. So it is without any hesitation that I recommend this book. The story is one of faith, courage, hope, and, above all, what can be achieved when we obey the Lord's call on our lives. From a missional perspective, Jeri's work in Romania is a milestone in the history of "business as mission." Many people talk about business as mission, but Jeri has done it. It is difficult to overstate the impact that Jeri and his co-workers have had on the town of Iasi. As a businessman now working in the field of missions, I challenge fellow businessmen to read this book with hearts open to what God can achieve through them for his Kingdom.

Piers van der Merwe, Director, Global Mission, Cedar Springs, Knoxville, Tennessee

Joining this whirlwind tour of Jeri's world, from Orange County, California to Ceausescu's concrete Romania in 1988, will jolt you more than a bad roller coaster. The juxtaposition of wealth and poverty, hardness and heart, torture and forgiveness, violence and peacemaking, and corruption and grace-giving make Jeri's journey more than a captivating read. It is a read-out of his heart, the gradual change over twenty years from a man driven to succeed in the financial world of Orange County, to one drawn to love by the person of Jesus. Read this 21st-century "conversion of Jeri"— missionary to the Romanians—alongside the 1st-century conversion of Paul— missionary to the Gentiles—for greater clarity.

Dr. Steve Hoke, Vice President, Training, CRM-US

Jeri Little's Romanian venture has changed the way I think of business in today's world. In what doubtless seemed a crazy venture, Jeri brought all of his entrepreneurial skills and passion to Iasi, Romania and there, against unimaginable business and political odds, built a series of lasting and successful businesses. Along the way, Jeri did the next irrational thing—he gave control of his venture, his people and its proceeds to God— offering them with an open hand to let God use them. And use them He has, in remarkable ways that stand as a testament to those businessmen and women who deep inside know that "there has to be more to this" as they think about how their life of work fits into the big picture. Jeri and Gloria's adventure for God is worth telling— and this book is worth reading.

Will Brooke, EVP and Managing Partner, Harbert Management Corporation, Birmingham, Alabama

Dedication

So many caring and committed people are such a vital part of this book that it would take another book to do them any justice.

I feel compelled, however, to dedicate what follows to the Lord Jesus Christ, because the tomb was empty, and every word of Scripture is true.

CONTENTS

This book is much more than the narrative of the production of a viable business as mission (BAM) in Romania. It's the story of the global, missional God wooing his people into sacrifice that becomes joy. The lead-up to the business is not wasted on the thoughtful reader, for it's the core of the heart story.

Yes, it takes a village to make a viable BAM truly work, but it also takes creative, gifted initiatives under the right leadership to make it last long-term. Jeri Little has done just that, and in the process given us a viable and vital model of what God may do around the world today in the creation of new mission models. These ventures require a broad missiology and a robust theology of vocation and work—all in the service of global mission. This happened in Romania, but has the potential of cascading creativity around the world, for those with the right commitments, honest-to-God tested experience, and the right skill-set and gift mix.

I personally wish Jeri and his team the best for a long-lasting set of enterprises that teach, model, and make legitimate profits for the Kingdom of Christ (a very good carpenter/home-builder himself) and in the process incarnate what it means to live fully and wholly in obedience to our unique Savior.

Three final thoughts. Firstly, who can forget Mircea and the price paid by those Romanian believers? Secondly, kudos to a mission agency, CRM, with a broadband capacity to listen to the missional Spirit of God at work today. Finally, this is a story much more about God than about BAM, more about God's passion for his church and the price faithful believers have paid already. And it's a human story of contextualization across the board; it's the church in Romania; it's a narrative of an entire family (Gloria, Marcus, and Trevor) on pilgrimage to the nations.

The book is marked by honesty, mistakes made, and challenges faced in the creation of authentic partnerships in order to make a viable mission business work.

William D. Taylor, Ph.D.,
Global Ambassador, World Evangelical Alliance and the Mission Commission

For some time now, many have suggested that I commit to paper a faithful rendering of some of the remarkable events that have taken place in my life and in the country of Romania over the past thirty years. It has been my privilege to speak, often and passionately, on this subject to a variety of church audiences large and small. I have demurred until now, however, when asked to write the full story of all I have witnessed and experienced. To these entreaties, my stock response has invariably been, "the story is still being written." Recently, however, I have come to believe that the broader body of Christ might benefit from the telling of God's dealings in my life, particularly my years in Romania.

One singular aspect of this recounting is my rare good fortune to have been "loitering on the corner" at a pivotal crossroads in Romanian twentieth-century history. Having observed, I can now bear witness to a tiny fragment of the first hours of a new era. Collectively, what the Lord has shown me over these years has served to shape me. Consequently, this is an intensely personal account of God's extraordinary providence in the life of the least of His servants, as he served in an exciting and challenging time in history.

From early on in my young adult life, introducing the concept of "business as mission" became one of my primary goals. I discovered, eventually, that making my home in post-Communist Romania was the best way to live out this aspiration. Over the years, I have done my best to serve in Romania as the Lord has directed my steps. However, in my endeavors to assist the Romanian people, I have by no means served alone. To this cause, the Lord has recruited, mobilized, empowered, and inspired hundreds of His people. So this is their story as well; a mutual labor of love and faith. But above all, it is the Lord's story. To Him alone belong the inspired vision, the battles fought, and the victories won. The various heart-rending defeats encountered along the way belong solely to me. Most often, what God has accomplished has been in spite of, rather than the result of, my participation. My primary role has been simply to set the table and invite the guests to His bountiful banquet.

My single preoccupation in telling this story is to see the Lord glorified. My prayerful desire is to present an honest and steadfast account. I have been painstaking in my quest to recreate a sampling of the most exceptional details regarding all that has transpired in seeing God's Kingdom advanced. What follows, then, is a minute part of God's story, which has also come to define my own story.

Jeri Little

The Little family, 1995

1964	Ceasescu comes to power in Romania
October 1988	Jeri's first visit to Romania
September 1989	Jeri's second visit to Romania
November 1989	Fall of Berlin Wall
December 1989	Romanian revolution and execution of Ceausescu
December 1989	Jeri's third visit to Romania
October 1992	"FiloMarket" opens in Iasi
January 1993	The Little family moves to Romania
September 1993	"Lilies of the Field" store opens in Iasi
July 1994	Thrift store opens in Suceava
October 1994	"Gloria" store opens in Iasi
May 1997	"Little Texas" opens in Iasi
1998	Bed and breakfast rooms open
September 2000	First Real Estate Venture
Fall 2001	Hotel wing opens

Note
The names of some individuals have been altered to protect their identities.

Prologue: Mircea's story

Mircea Detesan

Mircea Detesan was a native of Turda, a town just south of the Transylvanian capital, Cluj. He had come to Christ at an early age, growing in faith and devotion to the Lord in the heart of the Communist era. As an adult, he became an influential Christian leader, known for his refusal to compromise on spiritual issues. His reputation and influence brought him under the scrutiny of the local secret police (Securitate). They prevented him, like so many others, from obtaining an apartment for himself, his wife Mioara, and their two young children. Mircea asked his superior when he might receive a salary increase so that he could afford an apartment for his family. The boss replied that Mircea must first "give up preaching the gospel." This was punishment for Mircea's refusal to join the Communist Party. The authorities forced Mircea and his family to live in one cramped room in his parents' tiny apartment. This continued for years while Mircea quietly, but selflessly, served God's church and spread the gospel. Like many other believers, he was a tireless laborer who took great personal risks for the cause of Christ. He was well acquainted with the dangers, but persevered in his life's calling, entrusting all things to the Lord.

In 1987, Romanians secretly began to whisper about the winds of change in other Communist countries. The Romanian regime, fearful of similar manifestations occurring in its own country, focused greater attention on the defiant Christians. The Communists had done a remarkable job of creating a society bereft of trust. It is estimated that one in four Romanians was some kind of government informer. The authorities asked Mircea to become such an informer, but he categorically refused. From then on, they and government informers routinely watched, followed, and reported on all of his actions. Finally, one day in late October 1989, the Securitate came for Mircea in his apartment room.

Two men took Mircea by car to the secret police headquarters downtown. In a small room there, the Securitate officers told Mircea, in no uncertain terms, that he was now to use his influence and knowledge of the "movement" as an informer against other Christian leaders. Mircea replied that he could never do such a thing. Upon hearing his refusal, the mood of his hosts turned menacing. They assured Mircea that he would in fact inform for them or face dire consequences. For the moment, those consequences remained undisclosed, but there was no mistaking the interrogators' meaning. Mircea clung to the truth found in Matthew 10:19–20: "But when they arrest you, do not worry about what to say or how to say it. At that time you will be given what to say, for it will not be you speaking, but the Spirit of your Father speaking through you."

As usual, the process began with a demand that Mircea write out a declaration full of lies, dictated by the interrogators. Mircea refused. The chief interrogator repeated the demand. Again Mircea refused to conform. Soon another man entered the room. He bound Mircea with his hands behind his back and made him lie on his stomach on the floor. The chief officer produced a hard rubber truncheon. He stood over Mircea, pulling his arms back in order to cause extreme pain, and repeated the demand. This time the officer asserted that if he did not comply immediately, Mircea would never again see his family. In agony from the strain on his arms and shoulders, Mircea replied through gritted teeth that he would not become an informer.

The officer began yelling and took off Mircea's shoes. He bound Mircea at the ankles, hoisted up his legs, and bent his back in an unnatural arc, causing excruciating pain. This made breathing almost impossible. The officer began to whip viciously the bottom of Mircea's feet with the rubber baton. Mircea felt searing pain rip through his body. He could only manage shallow breaths due to the restraints that constricted his breathing. With the next blow came the threat that they would kill Mircea if he did not comply. The assailant paused as if to allow him finally to acquiesce. Slowly Mircea craned his neck to address his attacker who stood leering over him. Mircea managed to say, "You might as well go ahead and kill me; I will never agree to do what you are demanding." (Nowhere in Matthew 10 are we told that the divinely given words will come without a cost.) At this, the officer resumed beating Mircea's bare feet with even heavier blows, bringing beads of sweat to the torturer's forehead. Aware of the clock on the wall, Mircea knew that the beating went on for some fifty minutes. At some point the hail of blows ceased. Semi-conscious, Mircea was only vaguely cognizant of the officer's departure from the room. He would return to administer a similar beating four more times that evening. Desperate to protect himself, Mircea tried unsuccessfully to curl his now badly swollen feet under his body. At one point he cried out, "Stop beating me like an animal! You have the power to kill me ... I will never give you what you want! Kill me, but I will not deny the truth!"

The officer handcuffed him to the table leg and again left the room. During this respite, Mircea meditated on his present predicament and immediate future. He prayed, "I thank You, Lord, that I am counted worthy to suffer for Your name. I am ready to meet You, Lord. I only ask that You take care of my wife and children." A strong feeling that it was a blessing and a privilege to die for the Lord filled Mircea. The final beating stopped at 8:30 p.m. At that same hour, Mircea's church had gathered and was holding a prayer vigil to lift him up before the Lord.

Mircea's father, a non-believer and devout member of the Communist Party, came to the police headquarters to inquire after his son. He pled with the tormentors, trying to appeal to any sense of humanity in them. Not surprisingly, the entreaty fell on deaf ears and hardened hearts.

At midnight, three officers again entered Mircea's room, one of whom was the regional head of security. They proceeded to warn Mircea, on pain of death, to tell no one about what had taken place. Mircea was then free to go, at least for the moment. Outside the police station, the city was dark. There were no taxis, buses, or trams running. Barefoot and wobbly, Mircea struggled to walk on his severely battered and swollen feet. He gingerly ambled to the adjacent park, taking a shortcut home. He was soon crawling on hands and knees due to the unbearable pain. He expected the authorities to follow him now that they had seen him leaving the police station alive.

Extremely slowly, Mircea made his way over the bridge beyond the park. It would take more than three hours for him to cover a distance that was normally no more than a twenty-minute stroll. Eventually, Mircea arrived home to his family, who were beside themselves with worry. Once inside their small room, he related all that had happened, adding the warning to tell no one.

Later that day, three officers again came to the house to take Mircea in for further "questioning." One of them had a gun. The second of the three was a heavy-set colonel, a high-school chum of Mircea's father. The third officer also knew his father from their days together at university. While Mircea dressed to be taken away, he told his father what had been done to him the night before. The colonel flatly denied this when pressed by Mircea's father. "No one touched him," was the officer's retort. Mircea, however, had shown his father the telltale marks on his feet and body.

Within minutes, Mircea was back in the same tiny room at headquarters and seated on a chair. The colonel proceeded to beat Mircea on the head. Then came the all-too-real threat, "I will crush your head and splatter your brains on the wall! We will kill you—you will not leave here alive!"

Mircea's father went to the General Secretary, whom he knew, begging to have the colonel stopped. The father threatened to douse himself with gasoline and set himself ablaze right in front of the police station. Someone made a telephone call. Soon after, Mircea was told that he was being released. They again sternly warned him to say nothing. "You must now be an informer," they said, as they kicked him against the wall for added emphasis.

The officer who had beaten Mircea on the head hissed at him, "Go, you garbage. In less than three months you will be no more! Your wife will go to another man and your children will be on the streets. Then you will know that in this country there is no god but the Communist government!" Little did he know that revolution would soon break out in Romania. The military would catch and arrest Ceausescu on December 22 and summarily execute him on Christmas Day.

In the months following the 1989 revolution, the newly appointed Department of Human Rights called on Mircea. They brought before the tribunal the three Securitate officers who had brutally tortured him. The officer who had beaten Mircea knelt before him on his knees and begged forgiveness. He was facing prison for his crimes. Mircea asked that the accused stand. He then reminded the miscreant of his insistence that Communism was the only god in Romania. Mircea now asked him to respond to a question, loudly, so all could hear: "Who is God in Romania?" There was a short pause before the accused replied, "Mr. Detesan, your God is the real God in Romania." Even so, Mircea knew that his former, now fallen, tormentor was not speaking from the heart.

They brought in the officer who had beaten the soles of Mircea's feet. They read a formal declaration of accusations against him. The judge now assured Mircea that at his word, he would condemn the man to seven years in prison. Mircea declared to all those assembled that he could not condemn the man. He had chosen forgiveness instead. He only asked that the government never again give him a similar position of authority. Perplexed, the judge insisted, "You have nothing to fear; there can be no reprisal. Just say the word and this court will condemn him. This is your chance for revenge." Mircea repeated the fact that he forgave the man. Now bewildered, the judge pressed, "Give me a reason why you would forgive this man."

Mircea shared that he was a preacher of the gospel of Jesus Christ. The gospel compelled believers to forgive their enemies. Mircea explained, "I preach forgiveness from Scripture. If I do not also live it in my life then my preaching is worthless." Mircea then quoted from Colossians 3:13: "... forgive whatever grievances you may have against one another ... Forgive as the Lord forgave you." Mircea concluded, saying, "Jesus forgave. Paul forgave. I must also forgive." Stunned and incredulous, the judge confessed, "You forgive, but I could not." The judge wanted nothing more than to be able to condemn the criminal awaiting final verdict out in the hall. He could not bring himself to believe that anyone could forgive such a depraved man. Together, Mircea and the judge went out to the colonel. In disgust, the judge told the colonel sternly, "You should take off Mircea's shoes and kiss the soles of his feet that you beat. I wanted you condemned for seven years, but this man forgives you."

Through Mircea's act of obedient faith, the former colonel and career criminal would go free that very day. Mircea had chosen grace. Mircea imitated Christ through Paul's instructions in Romans 12:17–19: "Do not repay anyone evil for evil ... Do not take revenge, my friends, but leave room for God's wrath, for it is written: 'It is mine to avenge ...' says the Lord." If Hebrews 11 were written today, surely Mircea (and many others like him) would be found listed among those "whose weakness was turned to strength" (v. 34) at the moment of testing. He would be mentioned as having been "commended for [his] faith" (v. 39).[1]

It was among anointed nationals like Mircea to whom the Lord would lead me to serve. The story that follows is how all of this came about as Romania struggled to rise from the ashes of Communist dictatorship. Through its telling, I have endeavored to relate the truth as objectively as possible. My desire is to see the Lord glorified for his unfailing faithfulness and provision on each step of the journey.

Note

1 The Lord wastes no experience. Years later, his faith strengthened by his wounds, Mircea brought healing to pastors in Vietnam. With the country still under Communist rule today, the authorities are able to persecute, beat, and imprison Vietnamese Christian leaders for their faith. Because Mircea "withstood the test" under trial, he has been totally accepted by these believers and shares a special bond of brotherhood with them. Through God's perfect and unseen plan, Mircea and I crossed paths. I was given the great ongoing privilege of rendering some small service to Mircea's ministry, as he lived to equip and disciple others who shared his painful story.

Humble beginnings

Growing up in southern California, I was raised, with my two older siblings, in a Christian home. My mother was a godly woman who fervently prayed for me. Through her influence, I came to a faith of sorts at the age of fourteen. From my father, I inherited a strong work ethic. During my senior year of high school in 1972, and continuing through my university years, I worked at Reuben's, an upscale Orange County dinner house. The fast-paced action with the diners particularly suited me. It quickly became apparent that I worked well with the public in a serving role. This was a good job for me: the money was adequate, the hours flexible, and the adrenaline rush at peak times fit my "need for speed."

Upon graduation in 1976 from California State University, Fullerton, Reuben's offered me a position as a management trainee. While I had enjoyed my part-time work there, I was aware of how devastating the long hours, late nights, and weekends were on family life. I had witnessed many marital train wrecks. No, the restaurant business was definitely not a long-term profession for me. I determined never again to work as a "merchant" selling clothes.

With no clear occupational goal in mind, I finally accepted a management trainee position with Buffum's, a fine-line department store chain. I would spend long hours doing inventory in the cavernous bowels of the basement at the corporate headquarters in Long Beach. I was in charge of merchandise returns for all thirteen branch stores. I counted socks by hand. I would count and recount thousands of pairs of men's ankle and mid-calf hosiery. At times, my boss allowed me to work on the floor in the Men's Department selling to customers. This part of my job was enjoyable and I seemed to have a knack for "moving the merch."

In less than a year, however, I found myself gazing vacantly out of the window of my shared second-story cubicle at the grimy urban sprawl below. I was growing increasingly envious of the broken and homeless men shuffling by. They appeared free to me, if not carefree. Clearly, it was time to find another career. At twenty-three I had already peaked, or rather, hit bottom. My older brother Jeff was now a Certified Public Accountant with one of the "Big Eight" firms. I seemed a dismal failure by comparison. To further complicate matters, during my formative years I had developed two persistent habits: eating three meals a day, and sleeping indoors. Both, I had come to discover, required more money than I was paid to count socks. One thing was certain: the clothing industry was not for me. I determined never again to work at selling clothing to the public.

Longing for a meaningful change, I decided to contact Mr. William K. Dix, the thirty-five-year-old Agency Manager for the New England Mutual Life Insurance Company. We set an evening appointment at his office. This was a mere three blocks from my tiny apartment complex where I moonlighted, collecting rents and mowing lawns—anything to make ends meet. Arriving in the foyer of the New England Mutual promptly at 6 p.m., I noticed my name in white letters on the agency billboard. I was impressed. Mr. Dix (who insisted that I call him Bill) warmly greeted me and began to share about the insurance business. He pointed out that this was the one business that paid a man exactly what he was worth. He offhandedly added that most people could not afford to live on so little. Despite this subtle warning, I sensed that it was time to have my advancement determined solely by my willingness to apply myself (without the specter of petty corporate politics that I had experienced at Buffum's). To start with, I would borrow the credibility of the New England while developing my own over time. For the first six months or so, I would work for Bill. Then essentially I would have my own business. It all sounded good to me. Later that evening, back home in my little bungalow, I began to pray that the Lord would reveal His will in terms of my career direction. It was the first time since my conversion that I subjected a major life decision to God's leading. It was at once liberating and refreshing.

Two meetings and a battery of tests later, I was again sitting in Bill Dix's corner office. By this time, I felt certain that the Lord had chosen this field for my career. However, to my considerable consternation, instead of offering me a job, Bill launched into a recitation of my dismal test scores. The test questions ("Do you walk to work?" or "Do you carry your lunch?") were designed to indicate the relative likelihood of failure in the insurance business. Bill zeroed in on my rather mediocre results. "On this test we were looking for a score of, say fifteen. You scored a mere three,"

Bill disclosed with a definite wince. His demeanor struck me as that of a physician divulging the detection of terminal cancer. Caught off-balance, but undaunted, I paused for composure before plunging ahead. "Mr. Dix, I know that this is the career that God intends for me. I want it to be with the New England. However, if you don't hire me, I'll go down the street to your competitor and work for them." In response, Mr. Dix stared back at me in stony silence, weighing at length both my bravado and my flinty countenance. His face then brightened as he inquired, "Can you start on Monday?"

At the time of my transition to the New England, I was flat broke. My rent was overdue and my little Honda Civic was on empty. For a few days, there was no food in my refrigerator. Stubborn, youthful pride prevented me from simply showing up at my folks' home to borrow money or even to scrounge a home-cooked meal. Instinctively, I felt that this small trial was a rite of passage for me. I sensed that starting with absolutely nothing would serve me well in the years ahead. The Lord was showing me His providence in the midst of my current lack. At least, that is how I rationalized my hunger pangs.

I recall vividly the night at my apartment in November 1977 when I prayed to dedicate my new business to the Lord. This included a covenant to tithe on every penny I earned, however the Lord would bless my hard work. I reached for the kitchen telephone to make my first call as a New England Life agent. I put my hand to the plow and from then on worked with all the motivation and tenacity I could muster. I was cognizant that much of my drive was due to an unrelenting fear of failure. Success quite literally compelled me. Through backbreaking work and indefatigable determination, I managed somewhat to reign in my fears. Nonetheless, in the first several years, no amount of success could completely erase a lingering sense of looming financial ruin.

At the precise moment when my career was taking off, I sensed the Lord revealing to me the young lady He had chosen for my wife. I had given up on dating some months before. Until then, I had managed to make an absolute disaster of many relationships. As a far too carnal Christian, I had followed my own selfish desires in this area. Finally, I made a covenant not to date anyone until the Lord made clear to me His choice of a wife. This was the second major life decision that I entrusted to His keeping.

Some months after this decision, a young coed in our church named Gloria, also active in the college/singles group, burst onto my radar screen. This seemed a bit strange to me, as we could not have been more different. I was a loud, outspoken clown. Gloria was shy and retiring. She was a self-described "wallflower." What attracted me was her quiet servanthood and godly demeanor. I made noise; she made a difference.

I confided to Marc LeFever, my best friend since childhood, my desire to ask Gloria out. He thought I was joking and quipped that I would have to do all of the talking on our date. Then I told him that Gloria was the one that I would marry. That really got his attention! I asked Gloria out over the weekend between my acceptance of the position with the New England and the Monday I was to begin my new career. To my vexation, she turned me down. Not allowing her to put me off, I reapplied for the following Saturday night. This time she accepted. Over dinner at a restaurant, we seemed to hit it off. She had me hooked and I thought she was at least interested. The next morning I picked her up for church. We were engaged three months later and married in January 1979. Gloria was the flesh-and-blood ministering angel God employed to begin transforming my shallow and shabby spiritual life. By His grace, I married well and greatly above me. My Proverbs 31 wife daily aided and guided me. I had dedicated my career path to the Lord from its genesis and Gloria was my God-given compass to keep me headed in the right direction.

Gloria gave birth to our first son, Marcus David, in August 1980. We named him Marcus after my friend Marc LeFever, who was killed earlier that year in a freak accident involving gunplay. In August 1983, Gloria gave birth to our second son, Trevor Jeffrey. I exulted in our two boys. The Lord had given us the Psalm 127:4 blessing: "Like arrows in the hands of a warrior are sons born in one's youth." We so wanted our boys to grow up in the knowledge of the Lord and to have a personal relationship with Him. As a father, I knew that my sons were my primary mission field and I strove to be a godly example for Marcus and Trevor to follow. In this I often failed, something that I continued to regret, but from which I could only hope to learn and grow.

Despite my worries to the contrary, I did in fact manage to stave off financial ruin in those early years with the New England. I do not even remember skipping a meal (something I would, no doubt, have benefited from, given my waistline). Each passing year brought greater success and more exciting challenges in the business. The first two years I spent primarily making cold calls ("hot knocks") and traipsing around apartment complexes, following up direct mail leads. Slowly, painstakingly, I managed to develop a client base of influential contacts. This led to a series of accounts with owners of small companies. After nearly three years of working sixty to seventy hours a week, I had all the work I could handle. The Lord had blessed me with a challenging, rewarding, and lucrative practice. By my late twenties, I felt I had attained success by the world's standards. However, as a young Christian husband, father of two, and aspiring entrepreneur, I increasingly wanted my life to transition from success to significance. I earnestly desired to attain this before I reached an age when all that would remain to enjoy was the past.

Search for a mission

1986–1987

Although grateful to God for my business success and ability to provide for my family, I had come to see how temporal and unfulfilling success was in and of itself. This led to my desire to use my growing business as a financial wellspring for the work of the Lord. I was soon launched on a spiritual journey to discover how best to go about this. Dan Dyk, a close friend and fellow church member at Orange Evangelical Free Church, mentored me in investing my resources for Kingdom purposes. (Both the process and the friendship continue to this day.) Dan advised me to give financially only to ministries that I was willing to devote time to as well. Choosing the right places in which to invest my time and my money was still a classic case of trial and error. This simply meant that I passed through many trials and erred often.

I began to discover opportunities in missions both locally and internationally, looking for other ways in which the Lord might employ my time and talents. I decided to have my secretary set lunch appointments with selected clients that I had known for some time. They were told that the purpose of the lunch was personal, not business. It was interesting to note that when you handled a person's investments and corporate benefits, you always had unfettered access to him or her. I used this opportunity to tell my clients about my faith and about what Christ meant to me.

If I had had to make a living solely as an evangelist, Gloria and the boys would have starved on my paltry wages. Thankfully, however, during the normal course of my business week, I was able routinely to meet with clients and colleagues to share my faith. I believe that two colleagues did in fact come to Christ partly through such lunch appointments.

In August 1987, I met and began to work with Tony Amaradio, one of the top brokers in the insurance industry. Tony was moving to Newport Beach from Michigan to set up a West Coast office. Now connected to the same agency, we began working together on a number of cases. Tony and his wife, Carin, soon became close friends of ours. The fact that they were also Christians made our times together, whether for business or pleasure, even more fun and fulfilling.

In a matter of just three months, my business mushroomed and I was working larger and more complicated cases with Tony. We meshed extremely well as a team, and in the years to come, Tony and Carin's influence on my family's life would deepen and reach far beyond the business arena. I closed out 1987 with by far my best year ever, garnering a number of awards from the agency. Much of this was due to Tony's expert tutelage. This was a golden era for me personally. I had a wonderful wife, two terrific sons, everything coming my way in business, and I was able to dabble in different ministry opportunities as they came along.

One example of this came at the end of 1987, when my mentor Dan Dyk suggested that we visit another foreign mission field. This time his vision was a trip to Poland. He thought it would be a good idea to carve out two weeks in our calendars for late October 1988.

This seemed but a mere stroke of the pen to me in January of that year, so I quickly agreed. I then proceeded to go about the business of handling my ever-expanding client base. I was committed with all of my heart to pursue the business and do the best job possible for my clients. I enjoyed it to the extent that I even resented the arrival of the weekend. Friday afternoon meant having to wait until Monday to do it all over again. I saw myself in this career for my entire life. I could not imagine any vocational pursuit that could be more exciting or rewarding. I pushed away any feelings that said that what I was doing was empty or shallow. After all, was I not using my money and time to invest in ministry?

Into the unknown

1988

With the advent of New Year 1988, I began to reflect more deeply on how I was living my life. I came to the realization that in all probability I would not fail in business. Irrational fear had been my constant companion for more than a decade, but now I could look back on a storybook beginning and ahead to a fairy-tale future. I had everything. God had blessed me beyond measure. Peering ahead, I saw the next ten years being very much like the preceding ten. I loved my work and tried to convince myself that I was doing enough for God's Kingdom by giving generously to missions and participating in ministry opportunities. However, if I was truly honest with myself, I could not totally bury the thought that my career still left me with a sense of emptiness. How could I have such contradictory feelings? Why these throbbing doubts about the very direction of my life?

I slowly came to face the fact that, for me, the verdict was in. I had hit the ceiling of self-actualization. I was astonished to discover that it was indeed a low ceiling. I was too young (only thirty-three) and it had all come so fast. Increasingly, I sensed that my destiny would not rise above the limited personal satisfaction that comes from success in the business world. This was at once a disturbing revelation and a terrifying specter. Was I truly anything more than the sum total of my business? I began to worry about what lay ahead for me in the distant future. For the time being, though, everything remained the same. Life still included tennis, family, church, and good friends; truly, anything I desired from life's bountiful bill of fare. Out there in the distance, however, was my trip to Poland. My mind began to ponder that rapidly approaching commitment and what it might mean for me.

About this time, perhaps mid-year, the Lord began to whisper the word "Romania" into my subconscious. Until now, Eastern Europe had been nothing more to me than a vast landmass between Western Europe and Russia. It seemed a shadowy piece of the globe whose map had been drawn and redrawn throughout its often bloody history at the whim of less-than-benevolent conquerors. I preferred Western Europe: Bavaria, not Bessarabia; Baden-Baden, not Bucharest. So why did I feel inextricably drawn to a specific country in Eastern Europe? Dan told me not to worry. Our plan was to go to Poland. Romania would just have to wait for another time. And that was the end of that.

During the dog days of that languid Californian summer, Dan and I met with the leaders of Church Resource Ministries (CRM). We would travel to Eastern Europe under their auspices, since they had Vienna-based staff ministering throughout the region. CRM was not new to me, as Gloria and I had supported one of the CRM staff couples who traveled in and out of what was then Czechoslovakia. CRM has a marvelous and God-honoring approach to ministry, which Pete McKenzie, one of the founders, described as wanting to "give birth and give it away." Its role is to help facilitate new ministries leading to new believers, new groups, new churches, and new leaders. The idea is not to control but to contribute to, encourage, release, and empower nationals in the vision that God has given them for His Kingdom.

I recall vividly the lunch meeting with Dan and the president of CRM, Sam Metcalf. Ten days was the maximum time that I wanted to be gone. But Sam pressed me, virtually insisting that Dan and I attend their staff conference in Berchtesgaden, Germany on the front end of the trip. I enjoy Bavaria as much as the next tourist, but I was convinced that I could not afford that much time away from my clients. Sam dismissed my objection offhandedly, asserting that money was the only thing I would lose by being away the extra time. He pronounced the word as if it was something unclean and unholy. I merely smiled to myself, thinking, "This guy has obviously never had to make it in the corporate arena!" I became convinced that Sam would never be someone to whom I could truly relate as a peer. I could not have been more mistaken. With extreme reluctance, I agreed to the extra time.

Some weeks passed. I kept hearing in my quiet times with the Lord that same whispered "Romania." I suggested to Sam that this might be the Lord impelling me to see that country in particular. Sam sternly cautioned that Romania was the worst of all Eastern European countries. Furthermore, it was the riskiest: "Best to avoid going there." So Poland would remain the plan. That was just as well. I was not interested in taking any unnecessary risks. I had just moved my family into a 5,000-square-foot, seven-bedroom cottage in Villa Park. I had for years dreamed of living in this high-priced area with its large luxury homes on quiet streets. Now my dream had come true. Gloria chose the house and I made the payments. The house even had a gigantic swimming pool and large private office for me.

We decided from the outset to use the house for ministry of sorts. The extra bedrooms quickly filled with an unwed mother from Brazil, a Talbot School of Theology student, a recovering alcoholic, a CRM communications staffer, and a series of more short-term lodgers. These folk were all a joy to have around. I was certain the Lord's will was for us to live in that house for the rest of our lives.

In September, less than two months before our trip, I read an article in *Time* magazine about Romania and the dictatorial regime of Nicolae Ceausescu. Ruling by fiat, he was apparently a human-rights violator of the first order. I read further about his reputed personality cult and tendency towards megalomania. Added to this, I observed from his picture that he would certainly earn a place on Mr. Blackwell's Top Ten Worst-Dressed List. This article is what first piqued my interest in the plight of the Romanian people. That and the recurring whisper from God. When I shared this again with Sam Metcalf, this time he too was convinced that we should go to Romania. From this point on, it was clear that I was destined to visit this country, wherever it was on the map. In need of a geography lesson, I decided that I had better consult my world atlas.

The week before we were due to depart for the CRM staff conference, I received my first "test." My company had decided to take part in an investment fair at the Anaheim Convention Center. It would coincide with the first weekend when I was to be away. All four partners in our deal had put up exhibition fees. We all had specific roles to fulfill at the fair. I immediately saw the time conflict and announced to my partners that I would drop out of CRM's staff conference. I unilaterally decided that I would catch up with the group in Vienna or Budapest.

In response, one of my good friends, Ken Lorenzini, also a partner in the deal, drew my attention to my "faith faux pas." "Didn't you make a commitment to go?" he rather pointedly queried. "Yes," I replied weakly. "What do you think you will lose by keeping your commitment?" he inquired, even more pointedly. This nailed me to the wall. Praise God! My partners all assured me that they would stand in the gap and that I should definitely travel as planned. It was a great blessing to work with like-minded believers who were not afraid to take me to task.

Consequently, the trip in its entirety was a go. After picking up our rental car in Munich, Dan Dyk and I drove through the breathtaking forests in the Bavarian countryside. Some hours later, we arrived at the hotel in Berchtesgaden. We checked into our rooms with some time to spare before dinner. The conference would officially open later that evening. I felt jet-lagged, homesick, and totally out of my element. Satan was making yet another run at doubt. Why had I come? What was the purpose in all this? Would it all just be a waste of energy, time, and money? Besides, the missionaries that I had met when growing up had left me with a rather skewed perspective on them and their world. Would I really be able to relate to them as we interacted over the next four days? This would be four whole days of meetings! I would sooner sip hemlock than attend a meeting.

After dinner, Dan and I ambled over to the salon where the evening meeting was to take place. Some pastor was to be speaking that night. I hoped to avoid falling into a jet-lag-induced slumber. Some twenty people were milling around waiting for the rest to drift in.

As I stood next to Dan, my attention was drawn to the shuffling approach of a rather unkempt, bespectacled man in his late thirties. His gait was uneven and his rumpled suit looked slept in. His hair was a mass of unruly locks falling across a rather cherubic face. He was laboring to carry a well-worn canvas shoulder bag while unsuccessfully balancing several dog-eared books, notes, and papers. Upon reaching the entryway of the salon, he paused and asked in a pronounced Southern accent, "Has anybody seen my hairbrush?" Incredulous, I whispered to Dan, "Who is that?" "That's our conference speaker," he replied matter-of-factly. Taken aback, I began to wonder how I would manage to sit through the several speaking sessions on the program.

Our speaker was formally introduced minutes later as he rose to address the fifty-some missionaries and guests gathered for the conference. Within moments, Pastor Ronnie Stevens held our assembly spellbound as the Lord spoke powerfully through him. He drew out amazing biblical insights, woven together with history and laced with incisive wit. Ronnie cast diamonds with both hands. I sat transfixed on the front row, totally absorbed. I had long forgotten my jet-lag. Ronnie was also a missionary, the pastor of the Munich International Church. His preaching forever changed my life that evening. For the first time, I came fully face to face with the character of Christ. Through that understanding came an intense desire to be more like Him. The fate of Ronnie's hairbrush, however, remains a mystery to this day. Thankfully, it did not diminish the profound effect of his teaching in any way.

I was in for further revelations regarding missions in general and missionaries in particular. In that Bavarian valley at the foot of Hitler's Berghof, I found myself surrounded by young people in vocational ministry who unquestionably could have been successful in any chosen field. They seemed to be the best and the brightest. This shattered my preconceived stereotype of missionaries. I felt humbled and inadequate in their orbit. These were the kinds of servants with whom I wanted to co-labor, of that I was certain. I just had no inkling as to how.

At one of the evening hot chocolate breaks, several of us sat together enjoying the quaint Black Forest ambiance and one another's company. I was learning about CRM, its people, its vision, and its organizational ethos. I liked what I saw. I said as much to the others at the table. But then Sam Metcalf accusingly suggested that if I were truly serious about my faith, I would walk away from my business and give myself to raising money for CRM. I just nodded slowly, noncommittally, while my mind screamed, "Fat chance!" Things began going a little too fast for me. I assuaged my vague sense of guilt with the thought that Sam was in the business of asking the outrageous from the unsuspecting, with no real hope that anyone would actually deign to do the unthinkable. As such, he was no doubt used to constant rejection. I drained the dregs of my hot cocoa in smug silence.

After the conference, we traveled by car from Bavaria to Vienna. Once there, we got the train to Budapest, where CRM had put in place a clandestine team in 1986. Crossing over the Danube, we made our way to the apartment of Rob and Lori Yackley, the couple who led the team in Budapest. From Budapest, Dan would travel with other CRM staff to Czechoslovakia. I would fly with CRM staffer Bob McCuistion the following day into Romania. Bob was an ex-search-and-rescue helicopter pilot-turned-missionary and exactly my age. Also planned to take us in was Pete McKenzie, a CRM leader and man of God to whom I felt immediately drawn at the conference. Completing our quintet would be Pastor Bill Hay and his wife, Cyndie, from Birmingham, Alabama. So it was to be five people in and five out, in five days. That was plan A.

That evening we traveled back across the Danube on the Lanchid (the Chain Bridge) to the Malev airline ticket office. Once at the ticket counter, we learned that there were only four remaining seats on the next morning's flight. I began to feel deflated at the thought that I had come so far, gotten so close, only to have something like a lack of seats prevent me from experiencing Romania. At that point, no other destination on the mission's map held the slightest allure for me. Pastor Hay helpfully suggested that Cyndie remain in Hungary. Oddly enough, she preferred shopping to dodging secret-police surveillance in Romania. To me, this was incomprehensible. I would have preferred a pistol-whipping to shopping. I gratefully accepted her selfless offer.

Late that night, Pete came down with a raging case of twenty-four-hour flu, so he would be unable to make the trip with us. In a further twist, I learned that I would not travel around Romania with Bob and Pastor Hay. They would be on a separate circuit. A local Romanian would accompany me on my trip.

We eventually landed in Bucharest and presented ourselves to the ubiquitous airport military personnel. They wore armbands that said "Anti-Terrorist." They performed the tedious task of searching our luggage with perfunctory aplomb. The guards also frowned a great deal. Outside the terminal we took a taxi, a Romanian-built Dacia (rhymes with "gotcha"), from the airport at Otopeni into the city proper. Bucharest was a mere one-hour flight yet some sixty years removed from Budapest. To me, it seemed that we had done an H. G. Wells in some kind of time machine.

In addition to the general dreariness of the cityscape, I was freezing, and it was only October. Led by Bob, we walked around the city in a meandering zigzag route. Soon we were ambling down a suburban residential street, making our way up the apartment block stairs at 4 Mozart Street. A couple in their mid-thirties, Mihai and Ana Ciopasiu, greeted us at the door. Once inside, I asked to use the restroom. I noticed that the bathtub was full of water. Obviously we had come at an inconvenient time and were interrupting their bath plans. The water, however, was cold. Back in the living room, we all introduced ourselves and Ana fed us a wholesome meal. We ended up staying the night, all three of us sleeping in one bed, with Bob snoring and me talking in my sleep.

The next morning, I learned that Romanians always filled their bathtubs because running water was only available a couple of hours per day. Often there was no hot water. Electricity was limited to one forty-watt bulb per room and had to be turned off completely in the evening. Television provided no escape. It consisted of four hours a day of Ceausescu's propaganda speeches and, on occasion, bad Russian cartoons. The stores appeared lacking in basic foodstuffs or other goods to buy. Queues for common essentials were long and everywhere. "We do not have enough food or heat, but we have our President," quipped Mihai, as he mocked Ceausescu.

We decided to tour around Bucharest before leaving on our circuit later that day. It appeared to us that the entire city had used the same architect. Huge, nondescript concrete structures passed as apartment buildings. The Communists designed them with nothing but right angles, leaving them neither stylish nor architecturally appealing. Hundreds of Bucharest's fine villas from a bygone era had been torn down to make way for high-density housing in this "workers' paradise."

Having arrived in the center of the city, we found ourselves outside the infamous Hotel Intercontinental. This was a twenty-some-story "luxury" hotel, decorated in typical Communist style. I can only describe the ambiance as gaudy, seedy, and a macabre example of bad Communist taste. For security reasons, Mihai had not accompanied us on our walking tour, so we felt at liberty to go into the restaurant for lunch. The yellowish-brown, multi-globed, suspended ceiling lights reminded me of biology class when we studied the ravaged alveoli of the lungs of a terminal smoker. The remainder of the decor was not nearly so fetching. We sat at a booth in the middle of the dining room. Our briefing in Budapest had included the fact that this hotel was "spook" central, supposedly right down to microphones in the ashtrays. Therefore, we could expect to be under surveillance. A stony-faced waiter took our order without betraying the slightest emotion. We simply pointed at certain menu items to indicate our choices. While waiting for the food to arrive, we prayed for the meal. Pastor Hay led us in a prayer with our eyes open, as our briefing had advised. The rumor was that the waiters were all Securitate informers. So we kept our conversation pure vanilla, feeling uneasy in such surroundings. Our eyes kept darting furtively about, taking stock of our fellow patrons. We judged that we were the only Americans in the room. Still waiting for lunch to appear, I made a visual survey of the room. It was impossible to miss the evil pall cast over the entire place.

The next day, Bob and Pastor Hay left on one train, Mihai and I on another. Although Mihai spoke some English, we did not talk on the train. It would have been too dangerous. We did sit together, however. In every city, I saw the ubiquitous ten-story apartment blocks that Mihai had called "vertical graves." This was part of the regime's effort to urbanize and control every aspect of life. At different points, we stopped to visit several Christian families. The families included as many as twelve children. Their lives seemed preoccupied with scratching out a meager existence. There were the telltale signs of life's arduous strain on their faces, but their eyes sparkled with the unmistakable joy that only comes from knowing God. I was captivated.

Mihai and I traveled northeast to a city called Suceava. By now, I was suffering from flu-like symptoms and needed some downtime. The temperature seemed to plummet and this California boy simply could not get warm. Nevertheless, I slogged on. I was seeing firsthand the plight of Christians in this surreal land. Romanians subsisted in a netherworld that denied them the opportunity to dream, to aspire, or even to hope.

Life in Ceausescu's Romania

Many Americans, myself included, were largely unaware of the plight of the Romanian people by the hand of Nicolae Ceausescu. In multiple ways, he single-handedly worked to destroy everything beautiful and worthwhile in the country. In the 1920s, people called Bucharest "Micul Paris,"—"Little Paris" or "Paris of the East." Upon taking power in 1964, however, Nicolae Ceausescu took it upon himself to bulldoze much of the historic, classical architecture, stately villas, and centuries-old national treasures that gave his country elegance and pride. He drained the country of its wealth and resources to feed his insatiable "edifice complex."

Construction cranes littered the Bucharest skyline; with grim humor, Romanians named these cranes the "national birds." He replaced the valuable historical structures with a city of concrete guaranteed to depress and discourage the spirits of the people. He called himself "the genius of the Carpathians" and the "Danube of thought," but his only thought appeared to be of himself and his own self-aggrandizement. In Bucharest alone, he displaced some 80,000 inhabitants to build his immense "People's Palace" and expansive mall in the style of the Parisian Champs Elysées.

While these events were taking place within Romania, the outside Western world remained cautiously optimistic about Ceausescu's rule. In 1968, Ceausescu stood before a carefully orchestrated throng of his countrymen and denounced the Soviet invasion of Prague that followed the period known as the "Prague Spring." To foreign political pundits, this appeared tantamount to a clear fissure in Romanian–Soviet relations. Later, Ceausescu would bask in his "fifteen minutes of fame" on the world stage as an arbiter of sorts in a potential crisis with Libya's Muammar-al-Gaddafi.

In the early 1970s, Nicolae and his wife, Elena, embarked on a quest to gain international attention through a series of Head of State visits. This included China, where the Chinese met them with a vast display of pageantry dwarfing even that of Nuremberg in the 1930s. This greatly impressed the Romanian potentates. Soon, however, Romanians at home were to be humiliated, as the appalling behavior of the Ceausescus tarnished the country's international image. On a state visit to France, Ceausescu and his entourage quite literally plundered their living quarters. Objects d'art, furnishings, bric-a-brac, as well as bathroom fixtures were purloined. Shocked, the French felt inclined to warn the Ceausescus' next scheduled host, Great Britain. In order to secure an enormous Romanian aircraft contract, Britain's Queen Mother had agreed, with extreme reticence, to receive the obscure miscreants. The British courted the couple with full pomp and circumstance. In the end, negotiations reduced the contract to a single aircraft, for which Ceausescu proposed to pay with peanuts. This led, not surprisingly, to a feeling of sour grapes by the British aircraft industry. On the other hand, the forewarning from the French spared the Crown the indignity of parting with any national treasures or royal knick-knacks due to the Ceausescus' penchant for swag-bag diplomacy.

Despite this behavior, the USA was still reluctant to criticize the Ceausescus. Successive US administrations embraced them because of Romania's refusal to toe the Moscow party line completely. During the Ceausescus' visits to Washington, the Americans showered them with gifts that included furs, diamonds, and even a Lincoln Continental. Nixon made a state visit to Romania. Then, when Ceausescu visited the USA during Carter's term, Carter praised the dictator for his dedication to human rights. All this while the US Ambassador to Romania, David Funderburke, repeatedly informed Washington of the egregious human-rights abuses perpetrated by Ceausescu against his own people! The authorities curiously ignored Ambassador Funderburke's diplomatic missives.

During one of the Ceausescus' state visits to the USA, they scheduled a stopover for shopping in New York. Angry Hungarian protestors demonstrated outside the Ceausescus' smart hotel. Their complaint was with the Romanian regime's harsh treatment of ethnic Hungarians in Transylvania. New York Mayor Ed Koch appeared on the scene, asking Ceausescu, in an accusing tone, whether or not the claims of the protestors were true. This line of inquiry trampled on accepted diplomatic protocol for visiting Heads of State. Ceausescu, through his interpreter, protested loudly against Koch addressing him in such a manner. Mayor Koch simply replied that they were in New York, where things were done differently. New Yorkers, it seemed, knew how to deal with human injustice and petty despots.

If the American public as a whole had been better informed, perhaps they would not have stood by while the Romanian people suffered under dismal conditions. Here were Cold War politics at their chilliest. Washington saw Romania as a moderate regime among the other staunch Soviet satellites. The USA was therefore disinclined to meddle in such petty domestic issues as, say, the suffering of the Romanians at the hands of their dictator. This is one reason why many Romanians declared that they "waited fifty years for the Americans to come." The American people were largely uninformed and unaware. The fault lay in part with the US administration's policy towards Romania and in part with the lack of global interest or accurate perspective by a major percentage of America's citizenry.

Perhaps American voices would have begun to cry out if they had known more about Ceausescu's brutal treatment of Christians. His regime used psychological forms of control and persecution to terrorize believers. It was not against the law to be a Christian; you did not conflict with the authorities until you decided that you wanted to be a difference-making Christian. Therein lay the rub for believers we knew, like Mihai, who was beaten like an animal. He, and many others, were intent on making just such a difference, and consequently paid a dear price. Authorities harassed children of church leaders in school; they also removed many leaders from their places of employment or denied them promotion. It was not uncommon for the regime to employ severe interrogations and even imprisonment. In one case, the young daughter of a prominent pastor suffered a nervous breakdown because of her "state-sponsored" ill treatment at school. In addition, it was not unheard of for Christian leaders to disappear mysteriously off the street without a trace, leaving loved ones to grieve in silent fear. This happened to Mircea Detesan, whose story was given at the start of this book. The Securitate systematically targeted Christian leaders. Routinely, key believers were put under surveillance, hounded, and threatened. Life in a closed society, honeycombed with informers, made taking the gospel forward a particularly costly undertaking. It was, however, this greater "cost of discipleship" that helped to spawn the spiritual fervency that I noticed during my pre-revolution travels to Romania.

Under Ceausescu's regime, life in general for the average Romanian was arduous, monitored, and centrally planned. Stores were typically bare and waiting in long queues for daily necessities was a way of life. Food was rationed, along with electricity, water, and gas. The macabre concept of urbanizing the masses, cramming them into large apartment complexes, was as much a stratagem for surveillance as it was methodical dehumanization. Informers were everywhere and ever vigilant for incriminating tidbits to pass on to the Securitate. The government closed the country to Westerners and it was illegal for a Romanian to have contact with someone from the outside. News of the world was centrally controlled, filtered, and spun to fit the regime's agenda. The regime told the populace that the West was evil and that life in Romania was better.

Not surprisingly, people adapted, and over the years life evolved within the confines of Romania's borders. Voices of dissent were present but quickly marginalized and discredited within societal norms that had come to seem logical. Peer pressure was a consistent and powerful psychological weapon deftly employed by the government. After all, people still aspired to advance and achieve within the structures that Communism had cunningly created. The larger post-World War II/Cold War arena that surrounded Romania geopolitically aided in the fostering of such tight controls in all aspects of life within its borders.

There was, at the same time, full employment. Unemployment in the West was grist for Ceausescu's propaganda mill. In Romania, the government gave everyone a job and paid all virtually the same wage. Over time, the work ethic was eroded and quality became lax as the labor force lacked motivation. Top specialists in technical fields might receive 10 per cent more in income than their lesser colleagues. There was the myth of a classless society that was typically Marxist in its origins. In reality, Romania also had its elite class, which was given privileges and "luxuries" denied to the masses. For example, only a few people had an automobile, generally the Romanian-made Dacia. The government touted the "workers' paradise," although the population was expected to toil in the fields on Saturdays and some Sundays. Most Romanians, however, could afford to dine out and go on weekend outings. Government-subsidized vacations could be booked at state-owned hotels on the Black Sea. Given the decades of such an artificially controlled economy, the transformation to a free market caught much of the population unprepared. After the revolution, having to compete and actually produce left many longing for the "good old days" under Ceausescu. The popular saying, "Ceausescu pretended to pay us so we pretended to work," is very revealing.

Into the night, into the future

October 1988

Mihai and I reached Suceava by train. After visiting several Christian families, we were driven back to the train station. Mihai would remain in Suceava with another brother, Aurel; I would take the train to another city alone. It was nearly midnight. We stood in the shadows on the platform waiting to board the train. It was not safe for us to be seen together. In the silent darkness between us, Mihai gazed straight ahead. He finally asked, "Will you help us?" My head was spinning from all I had witnessed over the past three days. I only managed to mumble something vague in reply. Then it was time to go, so I climbed aboard, fumbling to find my seat. It was dark in the station, dark on the platform, and dark on the train. In this, Romania was ever consistent.

The train lurched, lurched again, then strained to pull away from the only people I knew, and the only contacts I had, in Romania. This unsettling fact began to dawn on me as we sped through the Moldavian countryside. My compartment was full of passengers but devoid of light. I sensed rather than saw my fellow travelers. It was at this point that I began to chastise myself for having come on the trip. I was, after all, 7,500 miles from home. Furthermore, Gloria had no idea where I was and had no ability to contact me, nor I her. I was now alone on my way to Iasi (pronounced "Yosh"). The rhythmic clacking of the train on the tracks lulled me into ruminating as to why the Lord had brought me here. I had only been in the country for about three days but had still managed to put my new friends at risk. It was illegal for Romanians to have contact with Westerners, and we could not possibly know who might have seen us together. Nevertheless, the devoted Romanian believers had housed and hidden me. They had sacrificed their meager stores of food to feed and keep me, even exhausting their gasoline allotment to chauffeur me around. They had even insisted on paying for my train ticket! I had taken up their time and their treasure, and, I was certain, more than the limit of their goodwill. What a waste for them! Mihai's whispered entreaty now began to haunt me. What could I do? I was a fish out of water, and with each passing minute I became more convinced that I was nothing but a high-maintenance fraud.

Eventually, we reached Iasi, and it was time to climb off the train. Now what? I had no instructions, knew no one, and had no back-up plan. I did not even really know what "Plan A" had been in the first place.

I was unwittingly playing Inspector Clouseau in this cloak-and-dagger melodrama. CRM had probably not shared any germane intelligence with me as I was clearly expendable and probably not even considered trustworthy. I climbed down awkwardly in the dark and looked out at a sea of heads bobbing rhythmically as they made their way, as one, in one direction. I could just make out that they were moving towards some kind of building. "Probably the terminal," I reasoned. So I joined in step with the throng. I then began to panic about what I would do when I got there. My briefing in Budapest had instructed me not to speak with anyone, to avoid eye contact, and to act inconspicuously. So what would Inspector Clouseau do now?

The clue came in another thirty paces or so. But first, I came to realize the answer to a major question in life: Yes, I really was a coward. The terrible knot in my stomach confirmed this. This was a minor, but telling, point, given my current predicament. At that moment, someone behind me grabbed my right arm. I had just enough time to think about someone mugging me, arresting me, or both, when a husky voice close to my ear rasped, "Hello. I am Nelu. Are you Jeri?" I nodded meekly. Clearly, I stood out like a rodeo clown. The hand that belonged to the voice clasped tighter, steering me through the crowd and avoiding the terminal. We threaded through a parking lot and climbed into a waiting Dacia car. Soon we were racing through the streets of Iasi. In broken English, Nelu informed me that we were to rendezvous at another believer's apartment.

We reached Columnei Street, parked, and quickly darted into a darkened apartment entryway. Again, there was no light in the hallway, but Nelu knew the way and we entered a ground-floor apartment. In the living room, a Bible study had just ended. Present were Bob McCuistion, Pastor Hay, and perhaps six other "brothers." I was relieved and delighted to see them. My façade of machismo was making a comeback. I managed to refrain from mentioning my disturbing brush with cowardice.

We introduced ourselves and coffee was served. It struck me that, at any moment, the Securitate could burst in and arrest the brothers, as well as give us foreigners no end of grief. But the locals seemed unfazed by the inherent risk. Nelu and Danut, the two leaders, would drive us the next morning west to Cluj. Yet another Dacia automobile would carry us on our trip.

We slept in that same living room, leaving bright and early the next morning. This excursion from northeast to northwest Romania gave us the privilege of seeing the picturesque Transylvanian countryside. The autumnal forest was aflame with hues of rust, yellow, and burnt orange. A gleaming sun shimmered on the leaves as a gentle breeze meandered through the trees and lazily swept over the valleys. With great relish, Nelu pointed out the natural beauty of his native country. In this, the Romanians could take great pride.

We finally arrived in Cluj, the capital of Transylvania, just before sunset. We parked somewhat inconspicuously in the lot, a safe distance from the entrance to the hotel. Nelu and Danut planned later to attend a prayer meeting in Cluj, then drive all night back to Iasi. They would both be preaching in the three-hour morning worship service.

This deeply impressed me. In their place, I would have stayed over in Cluj and returned the following day. Such sacrifice of service came from a lifetime of truly paying a price for their faith. Their fervor was in stark contrast to my often cavalier attitude towards church, quiet times with God, and my walk with the Lord in general. Those accusing thoughts of guilt were again rearing their ugly and convicting heads.

Bob, Pastor Hay, and I wanted to give something to Nelu and Danut as a small token of our appreciation. Time was short, so Bob asked if the hotel might have a gift store. There was a "Dollar Store" in the lobby. Apparently, they only accepted Western currency in trade. I suggested that we all go in together so Nelu and Danut could shop for themselves, but somewhat sheepishly, Danut informed us that only foreigners could shop in the store. This violated all my inbred American notions of right and wrong. However, I said nothing. Bob and I entered the store and did our best to choose things that our Romanian brothers could not otherwise obtain. We emerged with two bags full of small canned hams, packets of coffee, chocolate, and some small toys for their children.

As we would be remaining at the hotel, we said our goodbyes in the car so as not to draw attention to ourselves. I felt a special bond with Nelu. He seemed to live his faith with total devotion, a modern-day first-century believer. No reserve, no regret, no retreat. Now I was leaving, perhaps never to see him again. It all struck me as sad and somehow final. This, then, was my first lesson in missions. Ministry would often mean separation. That fact would continue to punctuate my life as a consistent theme. I silently pondered how people who did this full-time dealt with the extremes of emotion they routinely encountered.

On the train the following morning, Bob, Pastor Hay, and I recounted the various episodes of our separate travels. Nothing was as it had seemed to me back in Berchtesgaden just five days earlier. That now seemed an age ago. My brief time in Romania and all that the Lord had shown me had changed my perspective. Soon we were pulling away from the Cluj train station and heading west. I felt as if we were returning to the present; the time machine in reverse. I will never forget the strange sensation as we crossed the border back into Hungary. The sun immediately began to shine. Bodily warmth returned. The sky was a cerulean blue instead of the drab gray over Romania's cityscape. Flocks of fluttering birds chirped merrily. The contrast between Romania and Hungary struck me as just that stark. Hungary was still Eastern Europe, another Communist country with a language I did not speak, yet compared with Romania, it felt more like Shangri-La.

The expulsive power of a new affection

November 1988

As I began my journey home that October 1988, my mind was whirling as it replayed vivid images of people and places I had encountered. I felt an oddly eclectic mix of emotions. The Romanians' plight saddened me. I was angry at the forces that had enslaved and impoverished them. I felt a strange aversion towards the government that treated them as no more than chattels. Mostly, a sense of helplessness to do anything to make a real difference on their behalf simply overwhelmed me.

Before flying to the USA, I telephoned Gloria. Relieved and suddenly homesick at the sound of her voice, I told her that I had much to share with her upon my return. To my surprise, she replied that she also had a great deal to tell me. It appeared that the Lord had been busily conspiring backstage to prepare Gloria as well for the next step in our lives.

I arrived home, and after putting the boys to bed, Gloria and I talked awhile. She shared with me how the Lord had used her quiet times in my absence to reveal that He was quite possibly leading us in a new direction. The next morning I was, as usual, up, dressed, and on my way to the office by 7 a.m. I made my customary stop at a bakery for coffee and a bran muffin. I felt sharp, wearing my favorite double-breasted suit, and ready to dive back into business. Everything seemed to be returning to normal. I was starting to think that perhaps the effect of this trip would pass and it would end up being nothing more than an interesting topic of discussion with our couples' group from church.

As I drove to the office, instead of singing along to the country music station, my mind kept harking back to Sam Metcalf's challenge to "give it all up and go raise money for CRM." That was followed by the voice of Mihai Ciopasiu: "Can you help us?" "Okay, Lord, I get it," I said aloud. I needed to put Romania front and center on my list of ministries to support from here on out. "Whew, glad that's over and decided." Now I could get back to my normal routine.

But it was no use. After a business lunch appointment, I drove home to talk to Gloria. I burst through the front door and found her standing in the living room of our big, new house. I could see the dizzying redecorating vision dancing in her eyes. I just stood there for a moment, my suit coat still on. She gave me a perplexed look and then asked why I was home in the middle of the day. Had I forgotten my briefcase? Was I sick? Had I eaten something too exotic in Romania? "No, no. I'm fine," I assured her. "Except I can't do this anymore," I blurted out. "Do what anymore?" she inquired, somewhat guardedly. "The business," I responded. "I just can't do the business anymore. The passion is gone," I clarified, my voice trailing off.

I went on to say that I wanted to raise money for CRM's ministry in Eastern Europe. I said that I needed to call "that Sam guy," the one I did not like very much. Maybe I could take him to lunch. As I headed for my private office just off the living room, Gloria called after me, "What does all this mean?" "I have absolutely no idea," I offered reassuringly, as I fumbled through my dog-eared phonebook for CRM's office number. From that point, each moment held new revelations for our immediate future. However, looking back in retrospect, everything that happened seemed to be a seamless series of perfectly natural life transactions. This, then, was the "expulsive power of a new affection" about which I had heard so much.

The secretary for CRM informed me that Sam was extremely busy and helpfully suggested that I schedule something for two weeks hence. I had made a handsome living gaining access to the CEOs of closely held companies, so I did not give up easily. Surely I could winkle out some immediate face time with the head of a mission agency. After some time, Sam came on the line and, after riffling through the pages of his appointment book, agreed to have lunch with me the next day. What a coup! I had lost the business passion, but not the business touch.

There ensued a series of meetings over the following two weeks, at which I kept offering my rather vague and dubious services in development while Sam scrambled to get a consensus from his board of directors. He also needed more in-depth intelligence on me from the acquaintances we had in common. He called in my good friend Dan Dyk to discuss the idea. Danny brought up my income and the amounts I gave yearly to missions. He pointed out that those funds would no longer be available for missions if I made this transition. Sam merely responded with a mixture of fascination and bemused incredulity. After this, I met a couple of CRM board members as well as the office staff. CRM had me take a battery of tests, not entirely unlike the ones I had taken all those years ago for Bill Dix and the New England. In those two weeks, I spent quite some time in the company of Sam Metcalf. I now had a growing admiration and appreciation for this man of God.

Naturally, Gloria was involved in all the excitement as well. Upon my return home, she had shared with me the glimpse of the future that the Lord had given her—tiny hints of what lay in store. She had been studying Genesis, and when she read and re-read Genesis 12:1, the Lord's command to Abraham resonated in her heart: "Leave your country, your people and your father's household and go to the land I will show you." For some time, Gloria meditated on that verse. Later, she was similarly transfixed by the words of Jesus in Luke 18:29-30: "… no one who has left home or wife or brothers or parents or children for the sake of the kingdom of God will fail to receive many times as much in this age and, in the age to come, eternal life."

Obviously, this was a God-orchestrated conspiracy perpetrated simultaneously on two continents. The lot and the dye were being cast that would ultimately throw us into the cosmic adventure of a lifetime. Gloria shared with me how the Lord had been moving her towards an understanding that our lives were about to go through some significant changes. Scripture had been the basis for her surety in the Lord's leading. This gave us both a sense of peace. Truly, His Word was relevant for us in each and every situation.

I offered CRM my voluntary services in raising money, questionable though they were. In response, Sam stopped by my house in Villa Park toting a towering stack of printouts, hot off the computer. "Okay, turkey, if you want to raise money for CRM, then start calling the donors on these lists and set up some appointments!" he said, plopping his burden down on the couch. "Leave next week open and strap on your track shoes," I countered. Well, at least the first part of my new assignment was suited to my gifts and talents. Sam had coached me on some buzzwords and "CRM-speak." So I morphed right into calling CRM donors, lining up appointments for the president. That was the end of November, so I reasoned that the timing was good for our purposes.

That next week filled with appointments. Everyone had been very gracious to find time for us. Morning, noon, and night we worked through the schedule, traveling to people's homes and offices. I felt I was doing something important. I enjoyed this kind of activity. Sam hated it. For Sam, fundraising was anathema. This no doubt made my enjoyment of it even more puzzling (and aggravating) to him. I thought we made a good team. Sam was well informed, engaging, and erudite. I just nodded a great deal and faked my part. Astonishingly, many people responded and made donations right on the spot. Others said they would pray about it and let us know before year end. This was strangely similar to my experience with clients funding their retirement plans, IRAs, etc., at each calendar year end. (Later, I learned that the resulting gifts to CRM were used to make up their nagging deficit.)

After finishing the schedule early one evening, Sam and I stopped at a restaurant for dinner. Over a basket of chicken tacos, Sam announced that CRM did indeed want me. He admitted, however, that my test scores did leave something to be desired. The results indicated that I was a "tenure risk," whatever that meant. More disturbing to me (and perhaps to Sam as well) was the fact that the test further underscored my "need for a lot of money to be happy." Those two revealing assertions aside, I was accepted into CRM's family as an associate staff member by early December.

What remained to be determined was exactly what this would mean in our private world. Gloria and I invited Sam and his wife, Patty, over to discuss the future of my working with CRM. It really had not been terribly difficult to juggle my various business demands with all of the appointments with Sam. Therefore, the plan was for me to stay in business and dish cases off to my key colleagues, thus freeing up large chunks of my time for CRM. I would be virtually self-supporting for the immediate future, leaving any modifications in lifestyle to the dictates of future circumstances and our consciences. The Lord would reveal to us whether we were to maintain the house in Villa Park, our condominium in Palm Desert, and our lifestyle in general.

Later that evening in our living room, Sam asked us somewhat pointedly if we thought we could eventually adjust to living on a very small salary. We felt certain that we could. The four of us then prayed for the Lord's leading in all that lay ahead. I sensed that Gloria and I had just taken an important step of faith into that second most dangerous place on earth, the center of God's will (anywhere else being the most dangerous place; I had learned that under Pastor Ronnie Steven's tutelage). As spiritual head of my household, I was now being required to live out my faith, one timorous baby-step at a time.

We later learned that, as they drove away from our house that December evening, Patty turned to Sam and said, "There is no way that Jeri and Gloria are going to give all that up and leave it behind!" There was more. Pete McKenzie, one of CRM's founders and director of their Eastern European teams, strongly advised Sam against recruiting me. Pete felt that the mere prospect that someone could raise money, at virtually no cost to CRM, was not in and of itself a compelling enough reason to hire him. In Romans, the apostle Paul speaks of our offering our bodies as a "living sacrifice." Pete contended that the problem with a living sacrifice was that it kept trying to crawl back off the altar. I was an Olympic gold-medal crawler. Furthermore, another piece of CRM lore has it that Pastor Ronnie Stevens also counseled that they not recruit me. I had shared with Ronnie the struggle with my lifelong nemesis, a flagrant temper, inherited from my father. Due to behavior unbecoming a Christian leader (primarily on the tennis court), I had resigned as an elder in my church a couple of years earlier, feeling that I needed to concentrate on overcoming that particular character weakness. I was making only marginal progress. I came to comprehend that "tenure risk" meant that I would cut and run when the going got tough.

The counsel from Pete McKenzie and Ronnie Stevens was at once godly, wise, and discerning. Consequently, only by the sovereignty and grace of God was I able to work with CRM in any capacity. I had a full set of Samsonite baggage from the past and it soon became apparent that I had brought little or nothing of real worth to CRM. However, once I did come on-board, Pete willingly reached out to support me in my desire to be transformed more into the image of Christ. I was going to be on the receiving end of some amazing grace from these godly men and women with whom I would now co-labor.

Gloria and I had sought the Lord's guidance for our transition to ministry. We were convinced of His leading. That decision had seemed easy compared with approaching others with the news. Tony Amaradio was my primary business associate and I wrestled in prayer with just how to break it to him. Not only had we become good friends and trusted partners, but Tony had come to rely on me somewhat to close all but the largest and most complicated cases. On those, I was his lieutenant and liaison with the client. We had made some big plans together. I was more than a little nervous about how he would respond to my announcement.

One early winter morning, over steaming paper cups of coffee in the basement café of our office building, I haltingly shared with Tony how my trip to Romania had impacted me. I went on to say that I knew the Lord was calling me to vocational ministry with CRM. Studying Tony's face, I braced myself for whatever would come next. Tony was silent for a long while before he reached across the table and shook my hand. All he said was, "You just let me know what you need and I am here for you." His response was both humbling and affirming. Tony will never know the extent to which he ministered to me that day. He was one of the most successful brokers in the business. It certainly was not as if his continued success, to any degree, depended on me. In the short run, however, his business might be a bit more problematic. Yet Tony released me from any guilt, freeing me to focus on a transition. From day one, I knew that he would be my staunch advocate in the business, and one who would watch my back.

God's inept smuggler

Winter 1989

My family was moving into uncharted waters. Together we sought the Lord for the changes we needed to make in terms of lifestyle and daily living. Thus began the faith-walk of trusting the Lord in every decision and holding all of our belongings with an open hand. I was all too aware of how often our possessions can become our possessors. Certainly, I had seen this trend over the years handling the personal investments of hundreds of clients. The world says, "You are what you have," while James 2:18 says, "You are what you do." Nevertheless, there were still some complicated issues. Due to the manner in which our home ministered to so many as a refuge, I felt conflict concerning where we should live. Added at the beginning of 1989, to my consternation, were some stark California real-estate factors. The market was in the tank and we had bought at its peak. We prayed that the Lord would give us clear guidance as to His will.

In mid-January, I was working on the corporate health benefits contract renewal for my largest client. It had been my client for four years, but I received word that it was going to renew with another broker. I joked that the new broker would make me a little "broker." I took this as a sign from the Lord that we were to sell our house. We listed it with the same agent, a member of our church, who had sold it to us just six months earlier. Seeing the writing on the wall, we listed our desert condominium as well. This coincided precisely with the worst real-estate market in memory.

I put out a fleece to the Lord, something I do rarely and always with a fair degree of trepidation. I asked the Lord to sell our house by June 30 and leave us with enough to move into a place where we could continue to have a bedroom for guests. Months passed. During this time, I worked feverishly, learning all about CRM, meeting people, traveling, and running my business by remote control.

My family had a tradition of taking annual vacations and I wanted this year to be no exception, especially as I had been away so much. The June deadline for my "fleece" was rapidly approaching, as was the date for our much-needed vacation. We would be borrowing my in-laws' motor home and heading out to Bryce and Zion, California. Our boys were only eight and five, yet we already had a treasure trove of vacation memories. I had arranged to keep in touch with our real-estate agent, Bill, while we were away. This proved difficult as we were often in the wilderness and telephones were not readily available. Nevertheless, I continued trusting the Lord to answer my prayer.

Early on the morning of June 30, I awoke in the motor home and announced to Gloria that we needed to get to a telephone. I was certain something had happened. The call to our real-estate agent from the pay telephone of a local diner used up a large handful of coins. Bill asked me where I had been. I told him we were in the middle of nowhere. He wanted to know if I had heard the news; I assured him that I had not. He then informed me of an offer on our house that had arrived just that morning. He went on to say it was a full price cash offer, with no contingency. Bill had been my agent for years so I did not hesitate to tell him that the offer was "in no way acceptable." There was dead silence on the other end of the line. I waited some seconds before reassuring him that I was only joking. Some moments later, Bill resumed a normal breathing pattern. This was a kind of "gallows humor" for sales people who live on straight commission. We all did it.

Bill then added that he had received another call; it appeared that an offer was pending on our desert property as well. The Lord, in dramatic fashion, was giving an eleventh-hour response to my faith fleece. We continued the balance of our vacation, the Lord reminding us that He was an incredible real-estate broker.

It would now be necessary to find smaller lodgings that better fit our new financial situation. We ended up buying the house right next door to Gloria's parents in Orange. It had been empty for well over five years. The owners had passed away and their daughter had never done anything with the place. The yard was a weed farm. The interior reeked after years of chain-smoking. Gloria rolled up her sleeves and embarked on turning the house into our home, as only she can do.

Just ahead of the close of escrow, I had a second trip to Romania scheduled. I would be taking in Tom Sachs, a good friend from Alabama and younger brother of one of our Villa Park lodgers. Part of my ministry was to introduce supporters to the various mission fields by organizing such junkets. I would be gone nearly five weeks. This meant that Gloria would be moving us from Villa Park to Orange without my help. The distance was only three miles, but such an undertaking was at best overwhelming, even if I had been around help. Gloria managed it all with aid from friends and family.

Given that this was to be my second trip "in-country," CRM naturally assumed that I was an expert in all the missionary spook stuff that was part of such a venture. We had learned that Mihai needed a VCR to play Christian videos for evangelistic purposes. In the States, that would have meant a quick trip to Circuit City. However, in those days, it was against the law for Romanians to have radios, tape recorders, cassette players, copy machines, typewriters, and the like. I planned to buy a European VCR in Germany on my way in. I then learned that CRM had no idea how to smuggle such things into the country. This was more than a bit deflating. Nevertheless, I knew I had to make the effort all the same. I still had Mihai's voice echoing in my head from that dark night at the Suceava train station.

Tom Sachs and I linked up in Vienna, continuing together on a Malev flight to Bucharest. During take-off, I had thoughts of how cool it was going to be to try to get the VCR (now in my hand luggage, unboxed, and wrapped in my coat) past security. However, ninety minutes later, upon final approach to Bucharest, I began to have an anxiety attack due to the fear welling up in me. The authorities catching us was an idea that was becoming a little too real. I looked over at Tom and shot him a confident nod that I felt no part of. When the wheels touched down, my stomach started doing back flips. In panic, I began toying with the idea of simply remaining on-board the airplane until it took off again. Where was the American Embassy from here?

"What now, Lord?" was the "scud prayer" I launched heavenward. I soon came to my senses regarding fleeing the country. In any case, I was not ready to face another of those awful box snacks that the airline had served on the flight in. So I leaned over to Tom and whispered that I would get off first and go through security ahead of him with the VCR. If anything happened to me, he was to get on the next airplane out to anywhere in the West. Ah, good plan! I had no idea what I was doing, but Tom was relying on me. I needed at least to feign a calm exterior. I would deal with the interior later, quite liberally, with Alka-Seltzer.

I entered the dimly lit terminal about midway back in the pack of newly arriving passengers. We passed through double doors leading to a room with long tables lined up in a row on either side. Security directed each person to the right or left towards the tables. There seemed to be dozens of security personnel riffling through baggage and asking invasive questions. Several of these uniformed soldiers sported machine guns casually slung over their shoulders. All the passengers had opened their hand baggage for close inspection. Most of those ahead of me had already removed several articles of clothing, undressing under the watchful eyes of the guards, who had scant regard for propriety based on gender. I knew at once that I could not submit to any such inspection. I kept moving forward towards what appeared to be the exit doors. These were clear on the other side of the room.

I willed myself to keep my gaze straight ahead, thus avoiding dreaded eye contact. As I drew near the doors opposite, I clutched my bag more tightly under my arm. I was thinking that this would be a good time to disappear, quite literally. I started through the doors and began to veer right. Just as I did this, a distinguished-looking officer of some sort caught my attention to my left. I knew he was of a higher rank due to his shoulder boards and scrambled-egg embroidery on the brim of his cap. I made the unbelievable blunder of making eye contact with him, then looking quickly away. What I saw in his eyes at that instant confirmed that he knew I was up to no good.

There was not even time to berate myself mentally for the transgression. I continued to put one foot in front of the other with my back now to the officer as I moved away from him and towards the exit to the street. I fully expected at any moment to feel a hand on my shoulder and a voice commanding me to step into a nearby interrogation room. Yet I made it to the glass doors that led to the street. I was amazed and a bit dazed. Once outside, I went to the curb where a taxi (yes, a Dacia) was awaiting a fare. The cabby got out of the car and asked in broken English whether or not I needed his services. I told him "yes" and asked him to wait a minute or two. Surprisingly enough, he seemed to understand.

A voice from behind, calling in my direction, caused me to turn around. It was a machine-gun-toting soldier. He pointed his gun at me. Suffice it to say he had my full attention. It was apparent that he wanted me to get in the taxi and go. I told him that I could not leave because I was waiting for my friend to come out. He went back to his post. I motioned to the driver that I was still his next fare. Soon the soldier was back. He came right up to me and pointed the machine gun at my ribs. His voice was a bit more insistent. I was to leave NOW. Removing the stale, half-eaten airline sandwich from my jacket pocket, I explained in rapid English that I could not leave because I was eating my lunch. I began munching on the sandwich, now regretting that I had brought only one packet of Alka-Seltzer.

Again the soldier moved off. However, within a couple of minutes he was back and even more menacing with his weapon. Choosing the path of caution, I jumped into the back of the taxi and instructed him to go forward about fifty yards and stop. We then waited what seemed like an hour but in reality was probably no more than ten minutes. Finally, Tom emerged from the terminal to the part of the sidewalk where I had just dined. I motioned to him from the cab. He raced over, still buttoning up his shirt, and crawled into the back seat next to me. I shouted for the driver to go.

I looked over at Tom and asked in exasperation, "Where have you been?" I told him I had been waiting for nearly half an hour. He explained, somewhat defensively, that he had been shuttled off to one of the rooms and made to strip down, while they went through every article in his luggage. He said that they had done the same to just about everyone. With a puzzled look on his face, he then asked how I got through security so fast. "I guess the Lord decided to make me invisible," was all I could think of to say, patting the VCR perched on my lap. I was certain at that moment that it was the only plausible explanation.

As Bob McCuistion had done with me on my first visit, it was now my turn to lead Tom on a circuitous route to our rendezvous with Mihai Ciopasiu at 4 Mozart Street. I had no idea whether or not someone was following us. It struck me that perhaps the authorities had allowed me to pass through security as some kind of sting operation. Was I inadvertently leading them to Mihai's? We approached Mihai's block and I had some difficulty determining exactly which set of apartments to enter. They all looked alike to me. On the third try, I guessed correctly. All pretense of not drawing attention to ourselves was gone, as we must have looked like a pair of lost tourists to any casual observer.

We knocked on Mihai's door and waited, but no one answered. I was not particularly concerned. After all, I had just dodged a bullet of sorts at the airport, so cooling our heels in the relative safety of an apartment staircase for a bit was no big stretch. Eventually, we heard someone coming up the stairs from outside. The clump of heavy footsteps heralded the arrival of a large man on the landing below. Perhaps someone had followed us after all. Now the unwanted visitor was on the stairs at our level, appraising us wordlessly as we nonchalantly moved aside to make way for him. The man was easily six foot three, 230 pounds, and with a dark beard. He looked like a refrigerator with ears. His face was impassive. Just as I was mulling over whether or not Tommy could take him, the stranger stopped in front of Mihai's door. He then pulled out a key, looked down at us, and silently cocked his head towards the door as if to confirm that we were waiting for Mihai. Tom and I nodded quickly and darted up the stairs, through the now-open apartment door.

Once inside, we learned that the man's name was Bogdan; he was the brother of Mihai's wife, Ana. Now that he was relaxed, a broad smile transformed his entire countenance. We relaxed as well. Bogdan was a believer and extremely involved in the potentially dangerous game with the authorities. Many like he and Mihai carried out the transporting of Bibles and other illegal Christian contraband. Suddenly I was grateful that I had not given in to my cowardly urge to remain on the airplane until it took off again. That thought reminded me of what we had in my bag. I waited until Mihai arrived a few minutes later to reveal the VCR and present it to them. With unconcealed fascination, both brothers thoughtfully appraised the taboo electronic wonder now sitting on the coffee table. I assured them it was of good quality, handing them the German-language instruction manual. Mihai then asked how we managed to get it through the rigorous security at the airport. I casually related the story. In response, they simply stared at each other in silent astonishment. The two sat there for some seconds just shaking their heads. Mihai then said that such a thing was impossible apart from a miracle of the Lord. Who was I to argue? My hands were still clammy from the adrenaline rush. They shared with us how the presence of this VCR would allow them to reach out to their neighbors with the gospel. They could now use the Christian videos that had previously been smuggled to them. The brothers had only lacked the equipment on which to play the tapes.

We spent the balance of our time in Romania visiting various ministries. We traveled to Ploiesti, Ajud, Suceava, and finally to Iasi. It turned out that Bogdan and Ana were the brother and sister of Nelu, who had driven us to Cluj on my first trip. I began to think that the Christian family tree in Romania had no branches, as everyone appeared related to everyone else. In Iasi, we visited Nelu. His wife, Amelia, and his two young daughters, Simona and Miriam, were delightful. We enjoyed a broken-English chat animated with sign language over strong Romanian coffee in their third-floor apartment. Dacia was the name of their neighborhood. Now where had I heard that word before?

Nelu was a man full of life who loved a good laugh and was probably the biggest risk-taker among the "brothers." He shared openly about life in Romania, as much as the language barrier would allow. He explained that Iasi was the capital of Moldavia, as well as the seat of Orthodoxy for the region. A large university city of some 400,000, Iasi was that week celebrating the opening of the new university year. President Nicolae Ceausescu was in town for the ceremonies. He and his wife Elena were academic wannabes. She had bullied and manipulated academia to become the recipient of a plethora of scholastic accolades from the Romanian scientific world. She rather easily accomplished this by surrounding herself with hand-chosen sycophants. Nicolae's presence in Iasi meant that all police, gendarmerie, and Securitate forces in the region had descended en masse for the festivities. Many citizens were required to line up on a prearranged parade route to pay homage to Ceausescu as his motorcade passed. The crowds were obliged to cheer and fawn on cue for the newsreels. The authorities frowned upon those who failed to do so.

While this town-wide travesty was taking place, we were at Nelu's apartment wondering how we would get to our train bound for Cluj. Nelu offered to drive us to the station. I was apprehensive about the consequences should we attract unwanted attention. Nelu's insistence, however, finally prevailed over my misgivings. After purchasing our tickets at the station, he joined us on the platform. The rail car was jammed with people. It would be an all-night train ride to Cluj. As the only tickets available were for standing, Nelu followed us onto the train in a vain effort to find us seats. We spoke in hushed tones, saying our goodbyes. The train whistle blew and the doors began to close. We exchanged hugs, then Nelu was gone. With a pained expression on his face, Tom asked me if we would ever see Nelu again. "Lord only knows," I responded with a husky throat. "Welcome to ministry in Romania, Tom." Ministry did in fact mean separation.

Our time in Romania convinced me that conditions there were worse than ever. Ceausescu was further tightening his iron grip on the twenty-three million people over whom he reigned. I was feeling inextricably drawn to play a more intentional role in serving our Romanian brothers and sisters in need. At the time, however, I had no practical idea how that might come about.

Judgment day

December 1989

> Prudence, indeed, will dictate that governments long established should not be changed for light and transient causes; and accordingly all experience hath shewn, that mankind are more disposed to suffer, while evils are sufferable, than to right themselves by abolishing the forms to which they are accustomed. But when a long train of abuses and usurpations, pursuing invariably the same object, evinces a design to reduce them under absolute Despotism, it is their right, it is their duty, to throw off such Government, and to provide new Guards for their future security. (Thomas Jefferson and others; from The Declaration of Independence)

In the autumn of 1989, the world looked on as momentous changes occurred with the dismantling of the Berlin Wall. A truly macabre way of life and politics since 1961 was ending. Given the staggering death toll of World War II, which served in one respect to usher in a post-war East–West polity, it was even more astonishing that the evil empire's demise took place virtually without bloodshed.

I was in Birmingham, Alabama for a couple of church mission conferences shortly afterwards. After I had addressed a group of about fifty people, someone asked if I believed that freedom would now come to Romania as it had elsewhere. Uncharacteristically taking a moment to weigh the question, my mind wandered back to all that I had seen of life in Romania just the month before. The faces of the Romanians I had encountered flashed before me. Finally, by way of response, I suggested that only through the shedding of blood could Romanians win their freedom. In the days after that talk, I remember feeling that my answer had been naïve or misguided, perhaps even needlessly dramatic. After all, what did I really know about Romania? What did I know of the plans of the Lord?

Several weeks later, the telephone rang at my home in Orange, California at about 5 a.m. on a December morning. Groggy from sleep, I pulled the receiver to my ear. On the other end of the line was an extremely agitated Tom Sachs. Nearly shouting, he was telling me to turn on CNN, as revolution had broken out and Romania was in flames. It was just a few days before Christmas. I spent much of that day glued to the television monitoring updates from several news channels.

Fighting was heavy in the capital, Bucharest. The revolution seemed to have first erupted in the western Romanian town of Timisoara. Reports, though sketchy, indicated that troops had killed many citizens. Initial estimates of the death toll, however, were wildly divergent. A major firefight was still in progress for control of the government. The raging battles focused on the state television and radio stations as well as the airport. This pitted the regular army against Ceausescu's elite Securitate forces.

Later it would become general knowledge that, in the first days of mass street protests by tens of thousands of Romanians, Ceausescu had told the army to fire on the citizenry. He had ordered the National Minister of Defense, General Vasile Milea, to carry out this odious decree. When the General subsequently refused, the authorities charged him with treason. On the morning of December 22, in an inner chamber at the Central Committee's Palace, the General suffered a single pistol shot wound to the chest.

This took place when he was reportedly alone, seated at the council table and on the telephone to his wife, Nicoleta. She claimed that the line went silent for a moment. There then followed the sound of a struggle, then of a single gunshot. Moments later, an officer spoke into the telephone, informing Mrs. Milea that her husband had taken his own life. However, in an age of misinformation, rumors were rife as to how Minister Milea did in fact die. A state-sanctioned autopsy was performed four days later, followed by several months of inquiry. At length, the death was officially ruled a suicide. Many of the surviving facts, as well as Defense Minister Milea's family, however, reported otherwise.

During that same December morning, back in Orange, California, I felt a strong compulsion to go to Romania. I should gather medicines and go. Quite simply, I felt impelled to make the trip. I shared this with Gloria and she counseled that we pray further about it. So we did, and the conviction remained. I got in touch with Dr. John Schmidt, a friend who for years had been involved in medical relief in different countries. Dr. Schmidt offered a large quantity of medicines that were on hand and, coincidentally, not yet earmarked for any particular project. Our house became the staging area for getting the medicines sorted and stuffed into twenty large bags. I had spoken to Sam Metcalf and shared with him what I intended doing. Obviously wary, he said he would make a few calls to CRM board members to seek a consensus.

I made a few calls of my own. One was to Bob McCuistion, now in Vienna. Bob agreed to go with me if I could get to him and if we could get into Romania. I kept working on the logistics of the trip with one eye on the television to catch the hourly news reports about the situation. I arranged for Sam to drive me to the airport in his station wagon, as I needed a large automobile to carry all of the medicine. Gloria would accompany me to the airport as well. It was a dizzying time for us. I knew unquestionably that the Lord wanted me to make the trip. It was by now just after Christmas. Those now in charge of Romania had summarily executed Nicolae Ceausescu, the failed former cobbler's apprentice, and his bride Elena by firing squad on December 25. Merry Christmas, Romania.

At first, it appeared doubtful that the twenty large bags and my luggage would fit in Sam's old Buick station wagon. As always, I relied on Gloria to supervise the spatial logistics. She was certain it would work and, under her guidance, we managed to wedge in the last canvas beg marked "Romanian Relief" and close the back hatch. Sam then proceeded to read me the riot act. He recounted his telephone calls to several board members—none were too keen on the idea of this trip. It was clear that Sam's neck was on the line. He assured me that he would shoot me if someone killed me in Romania. Had there not been enough gunplay already?

Deflated by such sobering talk, I was flooded with doubt about the wisdom of what now struck me as a fool's errand. My spirits were sinking as we pulled up curbside at Los Angeles International Airport (LAX). If Gloria had not stood by me, I would at that moment have instructed Sam to head back home. After all, we could always give the medicines back with no real harm done. But then the wise words of Pete McKenzie came to mind: "Never doubt in the darkness what the Lord has revealed to you in the light." That bit of wisdom was now being tested at the pointy end of the stick.

We quickly located two very large baggage trolleys, piling all of the bags onto them. Moving to the appropriate line, we slowly made our way to the agent at the check-in counter. In a perfunctory monotone, without looking up from her computer screen, she asked for the hundredth time that morning, "How many bags will you be checking in?" Somewhat sheepishly I responded, "Twenty-three." This got her attention. She gazed over the spectacles perched on the end of her nose to the two large mounds on the trolleys. Her face contorted into a "Do Not Disturb" sign. "But sir, you are limited to just two checked bags," she scolded. "I will have to charge you $100 for each additional piece," she added with practiced officious finality.

Doing the mental math, I realized that we had a big problem. "But you don't understand; this is all relief medicine that I am taking to Romania," I countered pitifully. The agent looked at me intently, obviously weighing the veracity of my assertion. Seeing the "Romanian Relief" stickers, she then gushed, "Oh, I am from Timisoara and I have been praying for my people. Let me get my supervisor!" Moments later, with no small degree of prompting by the Romanian ticket agent, now converted to our cause, the supervisor quickly assessed our predicament. She then declared that they would accept all of the bags at no additional charge!

Upon hearing this verdict, I cast a sideways glance at Sam, who merely raised both hands in mock surrender. "Just go! I will explain it all to the CRM board!" From that moment on, my second-guessing ceased. The nagging doubt melted before this obvious orchestration and provision from the Lord.

During the flight to Vienna, it struck me that I faced yet another obstacle. I began to ponder my lack of qualifications to dispense the medicines and the medical supplies, now safely stowed in the 747's belly. "One thing at a time," I cautioned myself. At the airport in Vienna, Bob was there to meet my plane. He greeted me with news both good and bad. The McCuistions had Dr. Tom Edwards and family as guests for the holidays. Tom was a specialist in internal diseases, studying French for an ultimate medical missions posting to the Ivory Coast. He had already agreed to accompany us to Romania for the proper distribution of the medicines. "What sovereign providence!" I reasoned. The bad news was that the Romanian authorities had closed the borders. No one could get in or out due to the continued, intense fighting. Bob had been in ongoing contact with Austrian Airlines throughout the day, trying to arrange seats on our flight to Bucharest.

Surely the Lord had not brought me this far only to let me be turned away at the last moment! We prayed together for the Lord's solution that night at the McCuistions' apartment. I felt suspended between two worlds. What was the point of my having come this far, only to turn around and go back to California? After dinner, the telephone rang and Bob took the call in his study. Several minutes later, he returned and explained that he had been on the telephone with Austrian Airlines. They had just reopened the airspace in Romania and the airline had reserved the last three tickets for us on the first morning flight. Furthermore, they would take all of our bags at no extra charge!

God had answered our prayers. I had never before seen such a movement of the Lord played out so dramatically in my life. This whole scenario had an otherworld quality to it. We were merely bit players, a supporting cast in the cosmic screenplay of God's theater. These were uncharted waters for me. I was a novice at having to rely so completely on the Lord for every moment. The McCuistions and the Edwards, career missionaries, seemed to handle it all as par for the course, just another day at the office. We again prayed for our trip that would begin the next morning. The faith displayed that night by these believers who had already given their lives in service to the Lord deeply moved me. Bob opened the Bible and shared several verses from Psalm 91. We claimed verse 11 for our trip: "For he will command his angels concerning you to guard you in all your ways." I knew that this was the main reason we felt no real fear in going to such a place at such a time.

Pastor Ronnie's words at the 1988 CRM staff conference came back to me. He had quoted Dietrich Bonhoeffer from *The Cost of Discipleship*, where Bonhoeffer asserted that when the Lord calls a man, he bids him "come and die." There is a death to self for all Christians, but for some, it means an even higher calling to martyrdom for the cause of Christ.

Watching the McCuistion family—Rachel, age nine, Anna, age six, and Vicki—say their goodbyes to Bob, I was suddenly grateful that I had already said mine to Marcus, Trevor, and Gloria. While ministry sometimes means risk, it always means surrender.

It was a short flight to Bucharest and we quickly saw it had snowed heavily overnight. A thick coat of pristine white blanketed the landscape. As we descended, I could see from my window seat a line of some ten large buses. These were full of what turned out to be army personnel arriving to reinforce the extreme perimeter of the airport. The army had dispatched them to repulse further assaults by remaining Securitate forces still desperately active in the area. I began to wonder just what we were getting ourselves into.

Of immediate concern was how in the world we were going to get all these bags through security. LAX and Vienna were one thing, but we were now in Romania. This being my third time in, I was now a grizzled, steely-eyed veteran. Right, I was still clueless. Somehow I knew that just pretending to disappear was not going to work this time. We arrived with all of our bags downstairs in the usual inspection area. Instantly I noticed a distinct lack of tension in the air. The overwhelming feeling of spiritual oppression was absent. In its place were smiling military guards, courteous greetings, and helpful airport personnel. In a few words, I explained that all twenty bags were "aid." The immediate response was that we could pass right through customs. We did not even have to specify the nature of the aid. I felt no remorse at avoiding the usual strip search.

Once upstairs, we made our way to the outer glass doors. Tom agreed to remain with the bags while Bob and I arranged transportation. Inside the upper terminal, there were several large-caliber machine nests with soldiers stationed at the ready. The large glass windows to the left and right told the story of fierce fighting that had taken place for control of the airport. Bullet holes riddled the windows and walls beyond. The army had strategically placed heavy steel plates in front of the machine-gun crews for protection. They appeared to be bracing themselves for another onslaught. It was now nearly sundown. I did not want to be out in the open when night fell. We secured the services of two Dacia taxicabs. After much stuffing and cramming, we managed to close the doors and drive away.

The snow was deep and pure white. I could only just see out the windshield through a tiny opening straight ahead. I found this amusing and chuckled to myself. Now that we had arrived, I was beginning to relax. We soon approached the main bridge that led to the city. As we started to cross it, the white snow suddenly turned to a deep crimson. Puzzled, I asked the driver, who spoke passable English, what that was. He explained that this was the sight of a major firefight between the army and Ceausescu's Securitate forces. The mass of bloodstained snow painted a riveting portrait of the ultimate price paid for control of the bridge and essential access to the airport. For the time being, the army was in the driver's seat.

The city was eerily quiet. From time to time, we heard the staccato crackle of nearby gunfire. We made our way to the Hotel Modern, which was anything but. I pulled out a fistful of lei to pay the driver. With a shrug, he pulled out a similar wad, as if to say that the money had no real value. He smiled. That smile again, the one I never saw on the face of unbelievers on previous trips. We checked in and stowed all our bags in our rooms. I slept fitfully that night, awakened often by sporadic gunfire that I heard through the closed windows.

The next morning we met in the dining room for breakfast. As veteran Eastern European travelers, we came equipped with our own instant coffee and tea bags. A bleary-eyed waiter in his mid-fifties finally appeared to take our order. The tin of instant coffee sat conspicuously on the table. We ordered three cups of hot water. Not long after, the waiter returned with the cups of hot water, which he set in front of us. He then produced an empty cup of his own, which he held out, wordlessly, waiting for us to give him a heaped spoon of our precious granules. Naturally, we obliged him. We managed to stifle the laugh we would share later over this humorous, but sadly revealing, little slice of Romanian life.

At a nearby table sat a bearded, burly Scotsman, complete with kilt and tam, which he wore tilted at a jaunty angle. Hearing our English, he made his way over to us. He had arrived with gifts to give children at several orphanages. We explained that we had brought in medicines. In a thick Scottish accent, he asked whether we could take some of our medicines to a certain orphanage with which he was connected. He quickly wrote down the street address and the director's name. He handed Tom the paper and then gave us a worn and weathered old Santa doll to give one of the children. With that, we were now committed to visit the orphanage.

It was time to make our way to Mihai Ciopasiu's. Since road workers had cleared only major thoroughfares of snow, we proceeded on foot in the general direction of his apartment. Not even the trams were running. In some places, snow was thigh deep as we plowed ahead single file. This proved to be quite a workout, taking far longer than we had anticipated. Bob had a small map of Bucharest, so he took the lead and did the navigating.

Our little expedition was woefully lacking any well-thought-out game plan. Our only hope was that Mihai was at home. We did not even want to speculate on whether or not he had been directly involved in the revolution. All we knew was that many had died in the melee. That fact was all the more real to me after having seen the bridge. We finally made it to Mihai and Ana's apartment. To our great relief, they were safe at home and in great spirits. Over Romanian coffee, Mihai began to relate to us, in broken English, the momentous events that had occurred in the preceding days in his beleaguered country.

The dictator's fall

December 1989

In the main square in downtown Bucharest, outside the Communist Party building, Ceausescu appeared before a huge, yet carefully staged throng. It was mid-December, but the weather was mild, and not much snow had fallen. This resulted in a larger-than-normal turnout. On the balcony above the multitude, the dictator droned on with his usual dogma, offering the same meaningless party platitudes. Perhaps emboldened by rumors of the startling events in other Eastern bloc countries, several in the crowd began to chant, "Bread, bread, bread!" Taken aback, Ceausescu waved his arm for them to desist. He became agitated, stammering. One of his security agents came to the podium and reported, "Securitate is coming." Sensing the crowd's unprecedented defiance, the dictator panicked and fled inside the building.

Nicolae's advisors suggested he go back to the crowd and make a conciliatory offer of better conditions. Later it appeared in the media that his wife Elena had told him to use the tanks in the square to run the people over—was this not the purpose for which tanks were created? Confusion and bedlam reigned in the party headquarters. Outside, the crowd grew increasingly vocal. Someone made the decision to distribute fresh oranges, seldom seen during a Romanian winter, to all those assembled. The crowd received the news with great enthusiasm. Unbeknown to them, the authorities had injected the oranges with a hallucinogenic drug. The crowd of tens of thousands consumed the fruit with great relish.

The Securitate had positioned forces in all of the buildings surrounding the large square. They waited, hidden behind the windows with a perfect line of fire to the people below. Meanwhile, Nicolae and Elena had gone to the roof and boarded a helicopter in an attempt to flee the country. At some point, Ceausescu gave an order to the Securitate forces to open fire on the unsuspecting crowd, many of which were now under the influence of the tainted fruit. Bursts of rapid fire from automatic weapons began their murderous rampage, and apparently several of the drugged victims opened their coats and shouted, "Shoot me, shoot me!" Willingly, the guns obliged them. At ground level in the square, it was absolute pandemonium as the people realized they had no place to hide from the shooting. The army situated themselves among the crowd, but no one gave them further orders. Historically, the regular army and the Securitate were adversarial branches of the armed services. Now was no different.

Most of those scrambling desperately to escape the deadly hail of Securitate bullets were young people under the age of twenty-five. Many fell wounded, some dying. The general in charge of the regular army finally gave the order for his forces to return fire on the Securitate. This ultimately turned the tide, as the Securitate began to sustain heavy casualties. The guns at last fell silent. This, then, would be the final winter of Romania's discontent. No one knows the exact death toll from the carnage of that day. Graveyards in Bucharest are full of the many buried dead. Small black and white photos adorn white marble crosses that stand as a testimony to the victims, now hailed as heroes, who died in the struggle for Romania to gain its freedom. Mihai Ciopasiu's brother was one of the surviving eyewitnesses to the slaughter in the square.

Ceausescu's helicopter never made it to the airport. The pilot supposedly faked engine failure and set down on a street rather than reach cruising altitude, where he risked radar detection and surface-to-air missiles. The Ceausescus fled the helicopter and commandeered a Dacia from an old and very startled Romanian couple. The army soon apprehended Nicolae and Elena and took them to a remote military installation. They billeted them there for several days. Later a hastily arranged secret tribunal tried the couple and recorded the event on film. The members of the court never appeared on camera. They found Nicolae and Elena guilty of, among other things, crimes against humanity. The couple refused to recognize the jurisdiction of the impromptu court, threatening them with severe reprisals once they regained control. The deposed couple spent much of their last three days constantly bickering between themselves. They remained recalcitrant, venomous, and foul-mouthed to the end. In the courtyard of the barracks where the army had held them, they were placed against a wall, their hands tied behind their backs. (Later reports said several hundred had volunteered for firing-squad duty.) The officer in charge ordered that Nicolae not be shot in the face. The people particularly hated Elena, however, and they did not spare her this nicety in the execution order. Several volleys of rifle fire rang out. An officer shouted, "No one else fire!" The firing squad came forward through a lingering cloud of rifle smoke. Someone then filmed Ceausescu at close range to give irrefutable proof that the dictator was in fact dead. The revolution had succeeded. It was Christmas Day 1989. The national television station broadcast the story for weeks after. It showed graphic pictures of the dictator and his wife immediately after the execution. One of the reasons for this type of broadcast was to convince remaining Securitate forces that further opposition was futile.[1]

Note

1 This brief account of the revolution is based on several conversations I had with people much more knowledgeable than I about what happened. In addition, I have recounted certain aspects from several written and film documentary resources I have studied over the years. In no way should readers consider this thumbnail sketch to be definitive; I cannot guarantee its absolute accurateness. It is worth noting that we will probably never fully know the precise causes of the revolution. I have spoken to Christians who are convinced the revolution was simply a movement of the Lord. Some have suspected that it was a manufactured regime change, with the CIA playing a role. Still others look to Moscow as the originator. Rather than plunge into a rabbit hole of conspiracy theories, I prefer to focus on the result of the revolution: primarily, freedom. A freedom that would include, but not be limited to, religious freedom.

Aftermath of the carnage

Mihai helped us to make some calls regarding the priceless medicines that we had brought. We wanted to distribute them personally to reliable and competent medical professionals. Mihai arranged several meetings with Romanian doctors and churches. I was a mere baggage handler and bystander to all of the "doc talk" between Tom and the Romanian medical professionals. In addition to seeing how much good the medicines would do in the weeks ahead, it became clear to me that the Lord had used them as a vehicle to bring me to Romania again. This time the Lord sunk the hook deep. My destiny seemed from then on inextricably entwined with that of ministry in Romania. We all felt incredibly privileged to be with our Romanian brothers at such a pivotal time in their history.

We decided to make a sincere effort to find the Scotsman's orphanage. Armed with the written address, we started in the direction he had indicated. With some help from a fellow pedestrian, we found our way to the appropriate location. It was a rather large, walled complex in a secluded neighborhood. We rang the bell several times and waited. Some minutes later a cleaning woman emerged from the front door, some fifty yards inside the gate. She was dressed in a white bathrobe and carried a homemade broom. She approached the gate and began talking in a questioning tone. We tried to make clear that we had a doctor with us and that we had brought some medicines for the children. We did not make much progress. This was obvious because the frightened woman kept inching back towards the door and further away from the gate. Then Tom had an idea; he produced from his backpack one of the sterilized syringes we had brought with us. This got the woman's attention. She came closer and seemed to be saying that the director was not there and that we should come back another day. It was now late in the day, so that appealed to us. Mihai had warned us not to be out in the dark, as snipers were still active in several parts of the city.

When we came back the next day, the director met us at the gate. She was at first highly skeptical. At this point, Americans were still unusual in

Romania. Tom spoke some French to her, after which she began to relax and warm to us. After a time, she invited us in. She explained that there was so much terrorist activity that the cleaning woman had assumed we were there to do them harm. She asked us at what hour we had come yesterday. When we answered, her eyes grew wide, and she exclaimed that immediately after that, a sniper had shot a street sweeper just outside their gate. We exchanged incredulous looks. It was the first time that I had ever felt nearly bulletproof, truly sensing God's presence and protection.

By now, the director appeared sufficiently reassured about our identity and intent. We showed her the things we had for the children. As expected, the syringes were like gold. She confided that they had been sharing needles among the orphans. She allowed us to see some of the children. They were very small, between three and seven years old. We were in a room with about twenty children, giving and receiving hugs. For all we knew, these children could have been the recipients of the best treatment in Romania. However, several had AIDS while others suffered from various other maladies. Many of them seemed malnourished; all of them just wanted to be loved. At this point, I was struggling and failing to maintain some semblance of composure. I could only think of Marcus and Trevor, my nine- and six-year-old boys. I ached to see them at that moment. The thought tortured me that any of these little ones could be one of my boys. The staff thanked us for the medicines, we said our goodbyes, and we left. I remained an emotional wreck for the balance of the day.

We finished our medical circuit and then puposefully began moving towards Victory Square (soon renamed Revolution Square). It was here that the main carnage had taken place. On the way, we observed many makeshift shrines with hundreds of candles, flowers, pictures, and written poems placed where Securitate forces had killed Romanian family members and friends. The relief and joy on the faces of the people seemed muted, incapable of overt expression. There was a kind of gentleness in their demeanor. Though they were silent, their manner seemed to show the depth of their gratitude to be free from a great evil. We were some of the first witnesses to this liberation.

At University Square, we passed by the Intercontinental Hotel. We stopped to examine the many bullet holes in the large windows of the ground floor restaurant where we had lunched a year earlier. It was now vacant. I wondered how many of the informers had survived the recent developments. We crossed Boulevard Magheru and made our way down side streets until we emerged near another hotel. The shootings had badly damaged the hotel's edifice, along with many of the adjacent buildings. Bullets and the resultant fires riddled and blackened the stucco. As we approached the main square, the narrow alley gave way to a great expanse that had been the scene of much bloodshed just a few days before. Although there was a foot of snow on the ground, hundreds of people were silently milling around, taking in the sights of the battle's aftermath. We joined the crowd's aimless, almost reverent, wandering. The beautifully ornate Student Library, opposite the palace, was a charred ruin. The revolution had demolished and burned out its ornate cupolas. Heaps of rubble and debris littered the ground below.

Romania had been liberated, at great cost to human life. It was the only country to experience bloodshed in overcoming the Communist era. Our time there had been brief, but the trip left an indelible imprint on all three of our lives. As we traveled to Vienna, I was able to telephone Gloria and let her know that all was well. All was well—and everything had changed. The trip had affected me deeply. Many months would pass before I was able to fully process and appreciate all that I had experienced.

Back in California, I resumed my duties as vice-president of development for CRM. By the end of 1990, however, I was convinced that what CRM needed was a strategic thinker in the role of development officer. CRM was expanding and I came to believe that my long-term contribution lay elsewhere within the CRM family. In January and May 1991, I again traveled to Romania. I led a medical team, took in a short-term missionary who stayed six months to teach English, and escorted other visitors to that mission field. I spent my time in the USA attending various mission conferences, and speaking and sharing in key churches in Memphis and Birmingham. I served as co-missions chairman in my home church in Orange. However, by mid-1991, I had begun to feel a degree of restlessness. I did not sense that my work fully engaged my energy, faculties, and passion. The combination of lack of training and my amateurish limitations was also beginning to take a toll.

On a trip after the revolution, Bob McCuistion again met with Mihai Ciopasiu. They spoke of the future and what the ministry most needed. Clearly, discipling and training leaders was of paramount importance. This had been Bob's forte all along. Mihai challenged Bob with these simple words: "If you loved us, Bob, you would come and live with us." Bob had a rather intense and heart-wrenching walk around Bucharest later that day. Back home in Vienna, he could not escape Mihai's heartfelt prompting and began to ask for confirmation from the Lord.

I traveled with Bob on his next trip to Romania. We met with Christian leaders in Bucharest and Iasi. Bob felt a clear call from the Lord that Iasi was the place for him and his family. He planned a trip to take his wife, Vicki, to visit. She needed time to get her arms around the thought of adapting to yet another culture and language. In 1986, they had taken the step of faith to transition from Birmingham, USA, to Vienna, Austria. That had proven to be a daunting challenge for their young family. Romania would represent some additional daily challenges not normally encountered in Western Europe. For instance, finding healthy food to eat or dealing with lack of electricity and heat would be major issues. But though it would mean new and greater sacrifices, Vicki also knew that it was the Lord's will for them to move to Iasi.

The Lord often uses our children to teach us more about Him and to underscore some marvelous new facet of His providence. When the McCuistion girls were in Iasi for the first time, Vicki experienced high anxiety about their initial perceptions. She saw the drab, the dirt, the muddy streets, and a city palette devoid of color. As these impressions were trickling through her troubled mind, she heard eight-year-old Anna exclaim, "Look, Mom! A rainbow!" Sure enough, the rain had stopped and the clouds had parted just enough to allow sunshine to bathe an oil-streaked mud puddle by the roadside, thus producing a perfect little rainbow. Vicki reasoned that if the girls could see rainbows in the mud, they could live in Romania.

The McCuistion family arrived in Romania during a fine Indian summer. Their first surprise came when Nelu showed them the apartment he had arranged for them. Their new home was on the third floor of one of the many large, nine-story buildings. This meant constant street noise; the clattering of the street trams mixed with the cacophony of high-density life. The stairway inside their building was pitch dark and reeked badly. In the winter, there would be little or no heat in the main room of the tiny four-room apartment. This all came as a hard shock to the McCuistions, but they ended up living in this apartment for the next three years. Their dedicated obedience to follow wherever the Lord led humbled Gloria and me.

Bob would be working primarily with Nelu, now the pastor of a new Brethren church plant in Iasi. Nelu and a handful of dedicated leaders had a grand vision to create the FiloCalia Christian Foundation in Iasi, with a center for studies and training. The foundation building would be an incubator for ministry. The advent of religious freedom had awakened a long-dormant edifice complex in most church leaders. The city had granted them land the year before, no small miracle in itself. They told us that they now needed $100,000 to build the shell of what was to be an enormous three-part structure. This would be home to a plethora of ministries for the next generation.

I worked all of January and February to raise funds for this project. CRM was still small enough that we had never raised more than $65,000 for any campaign, and that was exactly the amount to which CRM was in debt when I signed on. After we had spent much time in prayer, the Lord had raised the $65,000 in my first year to eradicate that burden.

With the help of many individuals and several supporting churches, we then managed to raise an additional $50,000 for Romania. This was quite a significant sum given CRM's donor base in those early days. I considered this a phenomenal accomplishment by the Lord. Now the question became how to get the cash to Iasi. After weighing and rejecting several truly absurd options, I came up with the idea to sew half the money into makeshift pockets of T-shirts. Sam Metcalf and I would wear these on our trip to Romania in March 1992. We were to visit the McCuistions and deliver the funds to FiloCalia. However, before we did this, we considered it prudent to speak with FiloCalia's board and reach agreement on how they planned to use the monies. After several hours of discussion, we unanimously agreed on how to move forward on the building project. Sam and I sensed that the Romanians had a good handle on what needed to be done to construct such an imposing building. That was the first and last prudent thing I remember about this building fiasco.

Through this money-smuggling scheme, I learned something about cash: carrying too much of it on my person causes me to sweat profusely. Consequently, my skin positively glistened non-stop from LAX to Bucharest. Sam and I both looked at least twenty-five pounds heavier with the bulky patch pockets, front and back, under our dress shirts. However, with much prayer and feigned passive demeanor, we managed to escape having our contraband cash for Christ confiscated.

The next day, at a meeting in an apartment Bob had rented as offices for the ministry (one reason why they needed a building), we met with the entire FiloCalia board. At this point, our Romanian brothers only hoped, but were not yet aware, that we came bearing cash gifts. Nelu proceeded to reiterate his vehement assurances that $100,000 would build the entire three-wing, five-story behemoth except for the interior finish work. Bob was our guy on the ground, a veteran missionary, and practically a legend within CRM. Therefore, we reasoned that if he approved of this, we were on solid ground. At the end of the meeting, Sam disclosed that by the grace of the Lord we had managed to raise $50,000. We then shared with the board members the fact that we had the money with us. We brought out the T-shirts, cut them open, and duly delivered the cash gift. My banknotes were ready to mildew, but I was able to account for all of them. It was only then that I stopped sweating.

I went with Nelu the next day as he excitedly began making preparations to purchase large quantities of building materials. I met with the general contractor whom Nelu had chosen for his honesty. His name was Gandac, the "Cockroach." His name alone should have at least given me a clue. The appearance of so much Western money on the local currency market over the next few weeks substantially skewed the exchange rates for a period of time. But overall, Sam and I felt satisfied we had accomplished a good deed. Only later did we realize that we had unwittingly helped the Romanians launch a large building project that they did not have the capability to complete. Years later, the building would remain unfinished, although it did serve the purpose of housing several different ministries.

In God's waiting room

April 1992

Upon my return from Romania, I became embroiled in a potentially lucrative business venture. My mentor Dan Dyk had gone into a new partnership with my friend Ken Lorenzini and with Bill Hemrick, another friend from our church. They had opened a small trading-card outlet in the retail market and had quickly moved to put together other card deals. Together the threesome developed an idea for a "country music" card with top music stars. My flexible schedule allowed me to lend support to the idea. My only qualification was the fact that I listened to a lot of country music. I was country when country was not cool. Bill and I traveled to Nashville, contracts in hand, to meet with the Country Music Association (CMA). We spent a great deal of time tramping up and down 16th Avenue, pitching the idea to the managers of the stars.

We had rented a booth at "FanFare," the annual country-music festival in Nashville, the previous year; we wanted to test the market with a package of prototype cards. I knew absolutely nothing about the card industry, but I had always been fair at one-on-one sales. Therefore, I was in the booth with Ken, Dan, and Bill, in addition to a couple of other partners. The idea was a hit. Consequently, Bill, Dan, and Ken, the "braintrust," worked on a whole new set of cards to bring to market. My time was divided, rather awkwardly, between development work for CRM, keeping my personal business going, and running errands for the card deal. Although fully engaged in my varied schedule, I sensed that I was really just in a holding pattern, awaiting my next assignment from the Lord.

The focus of my passion continued to be making a difference for Christ in Romania. By the spring of 1992, I began to sense that we needed to create some kind of viable in-country enterprise. It needed to be a business that would provide employment for Christians. It had to be a Christian touchpoint in the community. Furthermore, it was essential that the endeavor create profits for ministry. Beyond this vague initial concept, I was drawing a complete blank—so much for having a grand design.

On the trading-card front, I was getting pressure to go full-time on the "country card" deal. Our time in Nashville was capped with a signed contract with the CMA and most of the recording artists' managers. Bill calculated that the value of my percentage would approach $400,000. With that much money, he reasoned, I could donate more than ever to ministry. Tempting as it was, I knew that I did not have the freedom in the Lord to do whatever came my way. I had come to understand the concept of a bondservant that the apostle Paul had written about.

I began to suspect that the Lord might be stirring the pot once again. I could sense that our lives were about to take yet another radical turn. One evening in May, Gloria and I sat up talking in bed late into the night. I warned her against becoming too attached to anything around her. I was certain that life as we knew it was about to change completely. In my quiet times with the Lord, a picture of my next assignment had begun to emerge. The revelation was clear, concise, and simple. Seeing the vision become a reality, however, would be far more complicated.

On June 15, I announced to Gloria that the Lord had given me a vision to start three second-hand clothing stores in Iasi. She had almost as many questions about such an undertaking as I did. Some of these were: where would we find donated clothes in the USA? How would we transport them all the way to Iasi? Could we find a method of marketing the clothes once they were there? Would Romanians even be interested in buying used clothing from America? Good questions. The questions came easily. The answers would prove much harder to find.

I had my work cut out for me. However, more importantly, I now felt that I had clear instructions from the Lord. I had my mission. The details were up to the Lord as I moved out each day in faith. I continually prayed for guidance. In an attempt to acquire clothing, I decided to call my good friend Fred Judd, a layman in Pastor Bill Hay's church in Birmingham who had visited Romania in 1991. I asked him what he thought about a clothing drive to gather good used, donated clothing at their church, Covenant Presbyterian. We could ship any collected clothing to Iasi from there. Fred was for the idea and managed to get approval for our scheme from the Session (church elder board). Thus began the first in a never-ending series of escapades into which I would drag an unsuspecting Fred. In later years, I teased Fred that he used to have a life before he met me.

With our first clothing drive under way, I contacted Bob McCuistion in Iasi to run my idea past him. Bob recommended that I travel to Iasi to meet with the Romanians and present my plan. I knew that I needed to have a working agreement with the leaders there. I wanted their collaboration in this groundbreaking venture. Key nationals with whom Bob was working had formed the FiloCalia Foundation in 1991, and one of their fundamental ministry statutes included an economic component. Therefore, I was hopeful that they would be agreeable to my idea. I made flight arrangements for the end of July. The initial threads of our tiny enterprise were beginning to weave together. I still needed to have a solid idea of how we were going to get the goods to Iasi from Birmingham, an immediate and large challenge. I began calling around and eventually spoke to someone with "Food for the Hungry," a great ministry that feeds many worldwide. My contact helpfully mentioned that Dorcas Aid International ran clothing stores in many parts of the emerging world. He suggested that I talk with their director, Dirk Groot, but gave his location only as "somewhere in Holland." This seemed like a thin thread of intelligence to go on, but through God's providence, when I called Dorcas Aid's Battle Creek, Michigan office, Dirk Groot just happened to be there at that moment. This ended up being a very helpful contact in setting up the transportation of our clothing to Iasi. Dirk agreed to meet with me in their office in Andyk, Holland that summer.

In preparation for the trip, I decided to visit California-area thrift stores. I spoke with any of the owner/managers who would give me the time of day. To my surprise, when I explained what I was attempting, without exception everyone was more than gracious to share from his or her vast storehouse of experience. I learned enough to know that if we could get such goods into Romania, we had every reason to anticipate a warm and profitable reception. The realization of a clothing store in Iasi was becoming more tangible. My course from that moment was set in stone.

I now had to give a definitive answer to Bill Hemrick and my friends who were laboring so hard to put together the country card deal. They were all

Christians and thus understood my situation. However, their project was at a critical juncture and the pressure on them immense. They were receiving orders from national retailers and it was crunch time. The revealed will of the Lord for me was so strong that the goal of starting a used-clothing store in Iasi impelled me. This was to be my singular preoccupation. At the same time, I was aware that I was probably walking away from a several-hundred-thousand-dollar windfall. The cost of obedience seemed to be ratcheting upward.

At this point, I learned another lesson about how God had been preparing me for this next phase of my life. The Lord never wastes any experience. My one year spent working for Buffum's in the 1970s would now begin to pay handsome dividends. At last, my sock-counting experience would not go to waste. All I had learned at Buffum's I was now able to use on this new project.

After an informative and fruitful meeting with Dorcas Aid International in Holland, I traveled on to Iasi. I met with the key leaders of the FiloCalia Foundation to discuss my proposal. Bob McCuistion had enthusiastically embraced the idea. His approval was imperative as CRM country team leader. We met with Nelu, Bogdan (Nelu's brother), and Donel, a member of the foundation board. In laying out my plan, I told them that we would put up the money for the first container and provide the clothing. Their responsibility was to find appropriate store space, get all necessary approvals, and hire the right people. There was agreement that the community would receive the goods warmly. There was no second-hand clothing store of any kind in Iasi at that time. Ours would be the first.

During my flight back, the steps yet to come were foremost in my prayers. I suggested to the Lord that what He needed to do was find someone willing to move to Iasi for a time to get the store to sustained profitability. A Westerner was needed to help in the initial stages, as none of our Romanian partners had any practical merchandising experience. On the one hand, it struck me as strangely presumptive to be giving unbidden retail advice to the God of the universe. On the other hand, I did have a whole year's experience at counting socks. Supposedly, this gave me some sort of license to lecture the Lord of All. I was such a fool. Once I was home, I spoke to Gloria about the vague possibility that I might need to go to Iasi for a period of time to oversee this new undertaking. We agreed that we would remain open to whatever the Lord had in store.

The church in Birmingham was continuously gathering clothes, the Romanians had found store space in Iasi, and rudimentary renovations were under way. I lined up a shipping company to transport the goods to Rotterdam, from where Dorcas Aid would truck them to Iasi. I decided to provide the necessary start-up funds myself. That way, if I failed, I alone would sustain the loss. Three years earlier, CRM had launched another business venture based in Vienna. It was to be an import–export trial balloon. It ended up a valiant but unsuccessful $275,000 endeavor. All the start-up capital had been lost. This made me hypersensitive regarding other people's money connected to business ventures and ministry.

The target opening date for the store was set as October 30. I planned to leave for Iasi in early October to help with the final preparations. The twenty-foot container of clothes, donated from the church in Birmingham, was now steaming towards Rotterdam. I asked Gloria to accompany me on this trip. We had begun talking about our whole family moving to Romania. She was willing to move sight unseen, but I assured her that I was not willing to move her without her having the benefit of some see-touch-feel time. Therefore, we planned to travel together, with Gloria visiting a few days while I remained more than a month. This was to be our last fleece on making such a transition. If we felt the Lord continuing to lead us to Iasi, then we would make a definitive move with the whole family.

Armed with this bit of news, I telephoned Sam and asked him to meet me. His instinct and inside track with the Lord had foreseen what was up. He had sensed that we would be moving to Romania. Forearmed, he met me with a printed outline. Included in it was that I would be under Bob McCuistion's authority, learn the language, and actually raise some personal support before departure. Thus our "business as missions" venture would be based on the traditional supported missionary model. In this way, all hoped-for profits would be invested in Romanian ministry. Sam's instructions seemed entirely reasonable to me. I was, nonetheless, still a bit perplexed at Sam's ability to be several steps ahead of me.

Eastern approaches, Eastern addresses

September 1992

Gloria and I flew to Budapest, having decided to take the train from there to Iasi. At the Romanian border, Gloria took in the dreary sights from her window seat in our compartment. After a moment, she turned to me and pointed out the window. "Look," she exclaimed, "red roses!" There in a cracked concrete flower box on the platform was a bed of pretty red roses, Gloria's favorite flower. "You know," she continued, "if there are red roses in Romania, then I can live here." Just like that, the Lord turned our world inside out and upside down.

Arriving in Iasi, we first visited the space the Romanians had rented for our store. I had left the location and the logistics to them. The store was in a very old, tiny four-room house on a busy street. It sat above the street and had no place for parking. The cement stairway from the street was steep and uneven. Most commercial space was still government controlled. Getting permits, approvals, and so on, was a huge bureaucratic undertaking. A Syrian medical student privately owned this particular house. The approval process for the store was well under way. Whatever its glaring deficiencies, the space would ultimately have to serve our purposes.

Over the next couple of days, Gloria began to get the feel of the city. She met several of the Romanians with whom I had been working. Her time in Iasi was also an excellent opportunity to get better acquainted with Vicki McCuistion. After all, we were about to become teammates and we had everything to learn about adjusting to life in Romania. With our families having two children nearly the same ages, Vicki and Gloria had much in common. They hit it off straight away. We spent as much time as possible searching for an apartment to rent. I was uneasy about moving with no idea of where we would be living. However, the day came for Gloria to leave Iasi and we were still clueless as to our future lodgings. I would soon live the CRM adage that "wherever the Lord's will leads you, His grace will sustain you." Besides this, I had experientially come to know the Lord as the greatest real-estate broker on the planet.

Determined to escort her on at least part of her return journey, I took the train with Gloria back to Cluj, ten hours west towards the Hungarian border. Once there, we spent the night in the same hotel where Bob and I had shopped in the dollar store in 1988. So much had changed since then. Now anyone could buy goods in the tiny kiosk. Our accommodation was predictably drab, seedy, and vaguely pungent. The decor was right out of a 1950's "B" movie. No heat in the room or hot water to shower made for a fitful night of tossing and turning. Gloria was in tears, mulling over the prospect of traveling on alone and then enduring an additional month of separation. We lay there in the dark stillness, fully clothed and fully awake on our cramped, lumpy twin beds. I remember remarking that Romania could use a decent hotel. Tomorrow meant putting Gloria on a train by herself and waving goodbye as she pressed on to Budapest to catch her flight back to the USA. Once there, she would begin, alone again, the mammoth task of getting us ready for our transatlantic move. The things we missionaries do to our wives.

I arranged to ride back to Iasi with another American missionary. There was much I needed to do and only a short time in which to accomplish it all. The days ahead were filled with interviewing potential employees, all candidates from the FiloCalia church of which Nelu Chitescu was pastor. Another high priority was finding the right place for our family to live. I assumed this meant an apartment, so we scoured the want ads and dutifully hunted down the more promising leads. The apartment conditions were, to say the least, abysmal. Of all the places we visited, the one that stood out had five tiny rooms on the ninth floor of a building downtown. The apartment was uninhabitable. I got vertigo just looking down from the balcony to the street below. The crowning blow, however, was that the lift did not work. In its favor was the fact that it was in our price range.

Upon further reflection, Nelu came up with a different tactic. He placed an ad in the newspaper stating that someone sought lodgings and would pay in Western currency. One day, Nelu announced that we had an appointment to see a "villa." This meant any detached home at least two stories in height. I complained that I could not move to Iasi and live in a villa when everyone else lived in apartment blocks. Nelu countered that it would be rude and inconsiderate to cancel the appointment. So I reluctantly agreed to see the house. We drove up to the area of Iasi known as Copou, which was well forested and boasted many stately old homes. The lady of the house was a Mrs. Sriner. She met us at the gate and, when I shook her hand, I saw the Lord's provision in her gleaming eyes. I felt instantly that this was where my family would live.

Her son-in-law Romeo took us on a tour of the upstairs, which had a separate entrance. As you might expect in a villa, the rooms were spacious and had lots of natural light. More importantly, the Sriners had their own heating system, which would mean hot water every day. I nervously asked the price. Romeo indicated $195 per month. That was the price of the other apartments I had already seen, all the while hoping to avoid contracting a communicable disease. I worried that this was the price per room, but Romeo reassured me that $195 was the total monthly rent.

I thought this was too good to be true and waited for the catch. Perhaps we would have to allow a family of gypsies to lodge with us on weekends. Or maybe our two growing boys would make too much noise for them. Or maybe it would be problematic that I did not want to begin paying rent before year end. Romeo responded that they loved children, and given that it was already mid-October, they could wait until January 1 for the rent. Every other landlord had insisted on a full year of rent in advance; I stated somewhat pointedly that I preferred to pay monthly. Romeo readily agreed. Furthermore, he offered to make the space available right away for any renovation I would like done. The house even came with a garage for my old car that we would ship over. Now I really had mixed feelings. I asked for time to think about it and get back to them.

We bid them good day and got back in the car. Despite my initial feelings, I told Nelu that there was no way I could accept the Sriners' offer. The place was too nice. What would everyone say? Nelu said simply that this home was a special gift from the Lord and that I must accept it. He had never seen anything like it, either. Later that day, he called the Sriners back and we closed the deal. The McCuistions had been hosting me for more than two weeks and I was anxious to give them a break, so I asked the Sriners if I might move in to get the feel of the place. Not at all surprisingly, they agreed. Without any signature or one cent changing hands, on the strength of a handshake, I was handed the key to an earthly version of one of the "many mansions" in my "Father's house."

For two weeks, I worked all day every day getting the store ready and returning alone each night to our new "home." Often I would not eat dinner, as I had only a tin of instant coffee, two spoons, and one coffee cup. I would read the Bible, listen to praise tapes on my Walkman, and then fall asleep on a kind of makeshift couch. I felt complete contentment with just these simple things. This was the sheer joy of the Shepherd of Psalm 23 comforting me. I was crossing the threshold of the next golden era in my life.

We hired Bogdan, my refrigerator-sized friend, to work on behalf of the store. Together we labored through all of the details to prepare for the arrival of the container from Andyk, Holland. We also hired five young women from the church. This was wise, as women tend to have a keener affinity than men for working with clothes. I sat through every employment interview. Nelu and Bogdan, of course, conducted these in Romanian. I just nodded, as if I understood what they were saying. At the end of each one, Nelu or Bogdan would turn to me to see if I had any questions for the applicant. I asked each in turn how she felt about working with a crazy American. I never got an answer, but all the girls got a big chuckle out of my quirky inquiry.

We had fervently prayed for the first clothing container to arrive in time and intact for our scheduled opening on Saturday, October 30. It reached Iasi just a couple of days before that date. The drivers were German. Gypsies in the town of Focsani accosted them when they stopped to sleep for the night in the cab of their gigantic Iveco truck. The drivers were rough and nervy guys, so they acquitted themselves handily, dispatching the brigands in a brief hand-to-hand encounter. One of the drivers had a swollen hand as a souvenir of their fisticuffs, but we had our precious cargo.

We offloaded the 1,500-odd bags of clothes into the store space. This was dirty, sweaty work, despite the cool autumn evening. Over the next two days, we opened every bag and sorted all the treasure. It was like a long string of Christmas mornings woven together. Included in this first container were clothing racks, hangers, and other accoutrements for our little store. We worked until nearly 10 p.m. that Friday evening painting the cases where we would display sweaters and ties. Finally, we were ready for the grand opening the next morning. I bid everyone goodnight as I walked down the street to hail a taxi back to my new digs.

Later that evening, as I lay on my couch/bed, sleep eluded me. I was ruminating on all that had transpired in the previous five months to bring me to this moment of introspective solitude. It was a pleasant evening and I had the window ajar, enjoying the night air. As if on the breeze, doubt and fear began to creep into my reverie. I began questioning my very reason for being in Iasi. Dread struck me like waves pounding surf and steadily eroding a shoreline. "What if no one comes to buy the clothes? What if all of this is for nothing? What will everyone say if this is a huge failure?" This was the voice of the accuser. I began to pray for release from this spiritual bludgeoning. The enemy was messing with me again. I got up and shut the window. Immediately, something like tranquility began to sweep over me. The hammer in my head ceased its relentless pounding. I drifted off to sleep, aching to see my wife and sons.

The next morning, the whole crew was beaming brightly as we shot a video of our new beginning. After a prayer of dedication, we opened the doors to an expectant mass of humanity eager to acquire the American treasures that awaited them in our tiny space. From 9 a.m. until 1 p.m., it was wall-to-wall "see-try-buy." A flood of pent-up consumer demand drowned out the previous night's doubt and dread. Our workers smiled at the patrons, cheerfully helped them, and showed them respect and patience—all novel experiences for Romanian customers. Their appreciation overflowed from the cash register. This was our "soft-opening," as we had only made one announcement in the Protestant churches. Almost all of these shoppers were Christians. Monday would be the big test with the quintessential "vox populi." Saturday's take dwarfed our projections. I was getting a crash course in Romanian retail jargon. Handling the money, I learned all the numbers. Ringing up sales, I learned all the clothing terminology. Trying to answer customers' frantic questions, I learned to smile like an idiot and ask for help.

Monday proved to be a carbon copy of Saturday, with even more people and longer hours. The God of the universe, swinging at the first pitch, had hit it out of the ballpark. This was a singular experience for everyone connected with the store. We could now look ahead to the challenge of keeping a steady supply of quality used clothing coming from the USA. One church would not be sufficient to meet that demand. There would be, however, time to address tomorrow's challenges fully. On this day, I was content to bask in the light of our Lord who fulfills His every promise. He is the one who does exceedingly more than we can ask for or hope.

I spent the next week working every day at the store, getting to know our employees, honing procedures, and learning the language. The Romanians were extremely gracious teachers. They seemed impressed that I genuinely desired to master their native tongue. By the end of each day, my tongue clung to the roof of my mouth. Getting back to my family, however, was the main focus on my mind.

From mid-November until Christmas, we were busy arranging for our move. We had decided to ship a container of our furniture and other accessories to Rotterdam, from where one of Dorcas Aid's trucks would bring them on to Iasi. Having some of our personal things would say "home" to our boys and perhaps be essential for a healthy transition.

Such adjustments come in all shapes and sizes. Sometimes they come with grief and tears. In early December, we were driving home from a family outing, and I was talking to Gloria while the boys were playing in the back seat. I happened to mention Max, our full-grown boxer. Max the "wonder dog"; Max, a member of the family. I said something about "when we get rid of Max." There was no way to take a dog to Romania. Now the heart-wrenching reality of our decision faced us. The connection between Trevor and Max was especially deep. When we arrived back home, Trevor went immediately to his room. Gloria sensed something was amiss. I wandered back to the boys' room, where my nine-year-old was in tears. What our move was going to mean to him personally struck him full force. Ministry meant separation for our children, too.

I held Trevor on my lap as bitter tears streamed down his face. I felt the pain so deeply that it was difficult to breathe. No words would come at first. I was praying that the Lord would come to my rescue so I could come to Trevor's. My little boy was brokenhearted and I was heartbroken for him. I gently began to tell him that, when it seems that the Lord wants to take something away from us that is very precious, it is because he wants to replace it with something even better. I then prayed silently to the Lord that it did not matter what that "something better" was, but I really needed Him to make good some day on my promise. I went on to reassure Trevor that, although we were moving, the family would always be together. I was certain I would never willingly split up my family. In the end, we were able to find a great home for Max on a farm where he was able to roam free and harass the barnyard animals to his heart's content. To our great relief, Trevor seemed to take this in his stride.

Rag business, Romanian style

January–February 1993

A s I would be leaving ahead of the family, I said my goodbyes over the course of the first few days of January 1993. My brother Jeff was supportive, but struggled with the idea of my being so far away for so long. To make it easier on family and close friends, I began answering their question of how long we would be gone by saying, "Two years." This made it easier for Gloria's parents as well as for my sister, Jill, who still grieved the loss of our mother from a heart attack in the summer of 1991. At a farewell lunch with a friend two years my senior, I gave the same two-year answer. He went on to reassure me that, if I did in fact come back after two years, I would still have a "couple" of good years left in me. A couple of good years left? I was only thirty-eight!

A week after I left the USA, I was reunited with my family at the airport in Budapest, Hungary. Our introduction to Romania would be by car on a harrowing five-hundred-mile road trip through a blinding snowstorm. With much prayer, seventeen hours after we left Budapest, we arrived safely in Iasi at the McCuistions' apartment.

Now that we had arrived, each morning I made my way to work at the store dubbed "FiloMarket." Our new apartment across town had been painted white since I had left in November. Gloria surveyed her future nest, making lists of what she would need to transform the four rooms into our home.

Our boys began home school. This was a totally new experience for us. Vicki and Gloria coordinated the curriculum we had brought from the USA. Rachel and Marcus were in the same grade, as were Anna and Trevor. Gloria had studied two years in the 1970s preparing to be a teacher in case she did not marry. Then, of course, I came along and changed all her plans. But she was well suited, gifted, really, to teach children and took to the task without skipping a beat. Our sons would embark on a wonderful odyssey of learning in an informal and familiar setting from the person who loved them as only a mother can. My role in their education was to serve as PE coach, bus driver, and spelling bee tutor.

One of the greatest blessings in our adjustment to Romanian life was Nelu Moraru, handyman extraordinaire. Nelu had coached me on what to bring for all of our appliances, machines, and such that make a house hum, whir, and buzz. Before everything was even unpacked, he had our washer and dryer up and running, and the same with the refrigerator, freezer, and bread machine (we needed to make our own). Within a month, Bob McCuistion and I had hired Nelu to work for us full-time. This suited both Nelu and us. He had worked in a factory where the conditions were appalling and the pay meager. His older colleagues thought he was crazy. Why would he give up the womb-to-tomb guarantees of a factory job in a workers' paradise for an uncertain future with a couple of Americans who might very well leave Romania at any time? Despite these questions, Nelu saw his future toiling on our behalf. He now had a decent job with some benefits to help provide for his wife, Maria, and four small children. Bob and I had the man to free us up so we could get on with our other, more urgent tasks. Nelu handled all extraneous aspects of Romanian life for us. This included car repair, registration, visas, household maintenance and repair, and a host of other things.

On the store front, I faced immediate challenges. In my absence, the crew had already lapsed into some bad habits. We made Bogdan, man of action, our "Man Friday" for the foundation, after his brief tenure as store manager. Working all day in the same location did not suit Bogdan's personality. In his stead, the foundation board appointed Dan Ciobanu to run things. We all attended the FiloCalia church, so relations were cordial. However, I soon began to see the folly of putting the wrong people in positions of responsibility and authority. Dan was a good man, but did not have a leadership bone in his body. Consequently, a showdown of sorts was looming on the horizon.

With our nest taking shape, no thanks to me, I was free to focus on the store. Sales were brisk, demand steady, and we were profitable right from the start. Early on, I began to get a grasp of the depth of the problem with personnel and human-resource management. This made me thankful, in retrospect, that I had not yet unveiled the broader vision that the Lord had given me. This was really to be a three-store "chain," if you will, by the end of two years. "One step at a time," I cautioned myself. There was much to be done in the days ahead. After nearly three months, the situation with Dan Ciobanu came to a head and I sat down with the key board members to discuss the future. I quite simply told them that I wanted a free hand to run the store the way I felt best. As it stood, within six months they would be out of business without really knowing what had hit them. To my relief, they unanimously agreed to my proposal.

Donel was a mature Christian in his early forties who served on the foundation board and as an elder in our church. I asked him to meet with Dan and me at the FiloCalia office. With Donel looking on, I began to explain to Dan that my job was to find the best position for each employee so that the store could run efficiently. I went into the kitchen and brought back a half glass of water (you can see where this is going). I set the glass on the desk in front of Dan. I went on to say that there are two kinds of people in the world: those who would see that glass as half-full, and those who would see it as half-empty (at this point Donel smiled knowingly and looked down at the floor). I then informed Dan that he was definitely not the former and as such would never be suited to manage people. Earlier, Donel had hit upon the idea of having Dan work in our new warehouse, so this is what I proposed to Dan. He readily accepted and I thus dodged a bullet of sorts.

At the store, I quickly settled into a daily routine. I was determined, as much as possible, to make fun out of the work. We closed for an hour at midday, a Romanian custom that I grew to appreciate. We used this time for eating together, reading the Bible, praying, and sharing. Just before re-opening, we brought out the new merchandise that had been prepared in the back room during the morning. We played Christian music on our cassette player for our customers, which they really enjoyed. At lunch, I would play some country music, much to the delight of the employees. We celebrated birthdays, anniversaries, and family news within our team to build camaraderie.

I worked six days a week at the store, Saturday being open only half a day. I closed the store on Sundays. We had a total of eight employees. The two Dans worked in the warehouse. Our store clerks were Carmen, Lena, Sylvia, Dana, Lenus, Mihaela, and Lara; all women, and all members of the same FiloCalia church where our family attended. Each one worked extremely hard, making the most of every garment that we pulled from the donated bags of clothing. We allowed our people to shop at the store, even giving them an employee discount. Each Sunday I would discreetly survey the congregation, recognizing our merchandise with all its bright patterns and jaunty ensembles adorning many of the faithful. "Our customers," I would think to myself with a sense of silent satisfaction.

Each day began at home with my language tutor, twenty-year-old Selena, coming to our house and giving me Romanian lessons. She wrote out cards with conjugated verbs and created exercises of sentences for me to complete. She also brought books, including a Romanian Bible, which we read together to increase my vocabulary. I worked with her for an hour before going to the store. Selena would then stay and tutor Gloria and the boys as a part of their school day.

Gloria, for her part, dived in with abandon at the task of home-schooling our two boys. Her day consisted of three to four hours of instruction and oversight of schoolwork, then busying herself with all of the housekeeping chores. Cooking was a bit of an adventure, since finding the necessary ingredients for whatever dish she had planned required considerable time and effort. Every meal had to be prepared entirely from scratch. She quickly learned the vocabulary necessary for a homemaker. I made myself available to her for the grocery shopping two to three times per week. Shopping for fresh vegetables and fruits took place at an outdoor market, all year long. I was amazed, but not surprised, with Gloria's swift and efficient adjustment to this new routine in Iasi.

Part of our family's immersion into the culture included standing in line for just about everything. Whether it was the post office, grocery store, pharmacy, or bank, there was always a queue. I could not help but remark on how dour and boring the work must have been for the average employee. When I reached the head of the line, employees would typically avoid eye contact with me and accede to my request in a totally perfunctory manner. I never saw a smile or a friendly gesture. In time, this weighed on me as I unwittingly began to adopt a similar demeanor as a customer. We chatted about this around our family dinner table. Our collective idea (I believe Marcus and Trevor suggested it) was to greet the functionary with a friendly "hello" and a smile. It was important to wait for them to make eye contact after the salutation and then proceed to make our request. I tried this first at the post office. During the previous few months, the same sullen-faced young woman had sold me stamps, only reluctantly surrendering the small jar of white glue to me so I could stick my stamps onto the envelopes. I dreaded every trip to the post office and the sticky-fingered ordeal of affixing my own stamps.

On my next outing, therefore, I was determined to try our new ploy. When I arrived at the front of the queue, I smiled broadly, offering a hearty "Good day" in my best Romanian accent. A moment later the woman looked up, wrinkling her brow at my beaming smile. She hesitated a moment before her countenance brightened and she flashed back a dazzling smile. As I paid for my stamps, she wished me a good day, smiling again. When I next visited, she noticed me several people back in the line. This time I had brought flowers (a Romanian gesture of friendship). She began nodding with a smile, ignoring whomever she was waiting on. Upon reaching the window, I offered the small bouquet of carnations, at which she beamed. After I bought my stamps, she helpfully told me to leave my letters with her, insisting that she would personally affix the stamps when time permitted. I thanked her as I left. From then on, I received no end of special treatment at the post office.

We used the same technique on the grocery clerk, bank teller, and everyone else we encountered. Without fail, we managed to win over each of the workaday-world Romanians with whom we interacted on a regular basis. We saw this as a "Missions 101" approach to our newly adopted community.

Our first drive across Romania in the winter of 1993 had seemed daunting, but such trips now became routine. The fact that I was driving a Western car, however, still made us something of a target for the local police in outlying villages. For the first year or so, when the man in uniform waved his reflective baton and stopped me, my stomach churned. Normally he followed this with a one-act melodrama, verbally abusing me and attempting to intimidate me. It was comical to see an officer of the law reveling in the local power base of his own little fiefdom, in which I played the role of subjugated serf. It was their one opportunity to lord something over a Westerner. At this, they mostly succeeded until I got a handle on the language. As my grasp of Romanian developed, to their considerable consternation, I began to respond in their mother tongue, in a confident tone and with no hint of being intimidated. Things then began to improve.

As a family, we remained committed to learning the Romanian language. Enriching this task was the sheer joy of embracing new customs and traditions, then integrating our unique contribution to the mix. Romanians always removed their shoes when entering someone's home. Then the host offered slippers to the guest. This appeared polite on the surface, but with time, we all began to see the wisdom of not having so much dirt tracked into the house. We soon purchased a basket of such slippers to keep by our front door.

When invited for a visit or a meal, a Romanian would never dare to arrive without having a small bouquet of flowers to offer the lady of the house. Having received an invitation to a Romanian home, I dutifully made for the open market to choose just the right floral expression of my appreciation. Having learned many of the numbers the first few days in the store, I felt adequately prepared to handle this.

In our last couple of years in California, we had enjoyed car telephones in both of our vehicles, as well as several in the house. We could call anywhere, anytime, and talk to anyone. Not so in Romania. We were privileged to have a fixed telephone in our rented space from day one, even though we shared a sort of party line with the Sriner family downstairs. Local calls were very straightforward. Of course, you could normally count on the operator listening in on your conversation. (An American family in Iasi was still quite a novelty.)

Long-distance telephoning, however, was something else altogether. You needed to telephone the female operator and place your request, giving her the number you wished to call. This challenged our fragile grasp of the rudiments of the Romanian language. The operator spoke rapidly and had no patience for repeating herself. If we were successful in voicing our request, the operator would then telephone us back when she had managed to place the call. This could take ten to twelve minutes, or ten to twelve hours. Several times the operator called at 2 a.m. to tell us that our call had gone through. At this point we would accept the call if it was urgent, or wearily cancel the request.

Lilies of the field

June–August 1993

In early June 1993, Gloria and I felt the need to take a weekend's spiritual retreat. We drove to Bucharest, some 250 miles south of Iasi, with reservations at a hotel in the center of the city. The first night was a restless one for me. My mind kept churning over the idea of opening a second store. I could see several obstacles and daunting logistical challenges. The next morning, Bible in hand, I wandered down to the lobby to have some quiet time with the Lord.

I began by praying that the Lord would sort out all the impressions that had been stirring in my mind during the sleepless night. I sensed that He was telling me to start the second store. We had experienced a period when we lacked a sufficient volume of goods in the small warehouse to supply our existing store fully. Consequently, I proceeded to explain to the Lord some of the facts about retailing. First, we needed to have a larger base of churches gathering clothes for us. Second, we had to be assured that we could receive goods year round, or we might find ourselves paying rent without sales to offset our overheads. I was certain that I had laid out an extremely convincing, point-by-point case, and this was even before the advent of PowerPoint. The burning impression remained, however. Since it appeared that I could not convince the Lord of the folly of His idea, I decided to change tactics. I asked Him to convince me, instead. I challenged Him to show me, in no uncertain terms, that now was the time for another store. My conditions included a guarantee from Scripture that we would have clothes in sufficient volume.

Opening my Bible totally at random, my eyes fell on a passage from Matthew 6. Verse 28 underscored the Lord's response to my inane lecture on the "rag" business: "And why do you worry about clothes? See how the lilies of the field grow. They do not labor or spin." Then verse 29: "Yet I tell you that not even Solomon in all his splendor was dressed like one of these." The Lord then taught me all about the "lilies of the field." I had read this passage on any number of previous occasions. I do not remember,

however, a specific lesson in retail inventory management from my previous reading. Now, however, it was in red letters, the very words of Jesus. Several times the Lord admonished me not to be worried, nor to concern myself with clothing. He would take care of that. My job was to move forward in obedience and stop doubting. Beyond that, and more profoundly, I was to stop viewing God's clear leading from a human perspective. Message received.

That next Monday, I breezed into the FiloCalia offices for a prearranged meeting with Donel. Over coffee, I announced that it was time for us to open the second store and that we were to name it "Criinii de pe Cimp" (Lilies of the Field). Donel asked why that name should be chosen; to which I responded, "Because God said so." After I went through my experience in the Word over the weekend with him, he readily agreed that we needed to find store space to rent and make all preparations for our second location. This energized us with a sense of expectation. Among other things, the second store would mean more new jobs and greater profits. From the beginning, we had kept a list of those who had sought employment but for whom we had had no more positions available. A job at FiloMarket was highly prized and greatly appreciated as a gift from God.

After doing an analysis of our costs and store overheads versus revenue, I came to the startling conclusion that we could no longer afford to ship clothes to Rotterdam and then truck them to Iasi. I was certain that we must attempt to ship from the USA all the way to the Romanian Black Sea port of Constanta. Our Romanian partners were not at all enthusiastic about my findings. They told me, "This is impossible. It cannot be done. The container will be stolen as there is a big Mafia at the port"—a significant point, to be sure. However, faced with the stark economic reality that we could not make money bringing in the clothes overland from Europe, I tried a different tack with our Romanian partners. I simply reminded them that we served a God who was bigger than any impossibility and shrewder than any Mafia minion. Since my arrival, it had seemed to me that every day in Romania began with an impossibility and ended with a movement of the Lord. One compelling reason, apart from the sovereignty of God, was that, if we were successful, our transport costs

would plummet by 60 per cent. After further discussion, they reluctantly agreed to try. Much prayer for the safekeeping of our forty-foot trial balloon marked the weeks leading up to the announcement of the container's arrival. I especially prayed that it would not go over like a lead balloon, as the stratagem was entirely my idea.

Donel and I traveled by car to Constanta in early August to submit the paperwork and receive the container from customs. The process was pure bureaucracy and a paper blizzard. To top it off, the temperature was in the mid-nineties and humid. We finally managed to extract the final stamp from the appropriate functionary with the help of our new freight forwarder. They then led us to the corresponding container number in a vast storage yard. This was definitely not the glamorous part of the fashion industry. Predictably, the container seal had already been broken. Just as predictably, we had zero recourse. It was now up to Donel and I to offload the goods by hand, all 1,500 bags.

We flagged down a lorry for hire and negotiated with the driver to truck our goods to Iasi. We then proceeded to unload one bag at a time into the back of the truck. We were not alone. The truck driver watched, seemingly fascinated by our toil and my grunting with each heave. It was easily 120 degrees in the rectangular metal box. Keeping the truck driver company on his faithful vigil was a youthful customs official, no doubt making sure that we did not steal any of our own goods. After thirty sweaty minutes with little result, I offered the driver money to help us with our task. After two counter offers, we reached an accord. This left the customs official jabbering non-stop about the poor quality of clothes we were bringing into his country. He kept up a constant barrage of invective to which I responded with far more tact than I felt. One bag burst open upon being hoisted and some of its contents toppled to the wooden floor of the container. Observing this, the official began ranting about how worthless the stained clothing would be now. I assured him that it would be washed before being sold.

At last, the task was completed. Donel and I emerged from the rectangular steel oven glistening with sweat, like horses that someone had ridden hard. It was agreed that we would pay the driver half of the money now and the balance when we met again in Iasi. As his truck and our

treasure rolled away, representing the next four months' wages and profits for our store, I was wondering if that was the last we would see of the driver. This truly was a risky business. We began praying for the truck's safe arrival in Iasi. Two days later, there was no small amount of celebrating among our little clan when we finally offloaded the entire transport into our own warehouse.

Our future now lay with shipping directly to Romania. The gamble had paid off. The risk taken had saved us a great deal of money. God had been gracious. Now, depending on where the clothes were gathered, the transport route would begin at either the port at Savannah, Georgia or Long Beach, California (if Long Beach, then the goods went through the Panama Canal and the Caribbean). Then they would travel across the Atlantic Ocean to Haifa, Israel where the container changed ships. Leaving Haifa, the new ship traversed the Mediterranean through the Dardanelles to the Black Sea, then northwest to the port of Constanta. This was a multinational voyage requiring some four to six weeks. From the beginning, despite our lack of experience, the Lord had shown us the way forward as we took each tiny step of faith.

❝ Thorny issues

Mid-1993

Following the revolution, most Romanian churches awoke with a desire to build. Pastors with a vision could now give full vent to their building inclination. It became an overnight mania. Long denied them, it was now possible, if they had the funds. In early 1992, as already mentioned, FiloCalia had embarked on constructing a mammoth ministry building complex on land granted to them by City Hall. As I mentioned earlier, in March of that year, Sam and I had brought in $50,000 to help build the center, money raised over several months. Unfortunately, instead of completing half of the entire structure as they told us they could, they ended up with only part of the foundation and a fraction of the main staircase. There was no fiscal impropriety, but unscrupulous people had victimized an inexperienced and naïve Nelu Chitescu, our pastor.

The advent of our arrival in Iasi in 1993 signaled my shift away from fundraising in the USA in general and for the building in particular. I wanted to focus instead on the store and earning funds for ministry in Romania. This was the vision the Lord had given me. Not unexpectedly, Nelu did not meet this change with grace and understanding. I was repeatedly told that the nearly $7,000 of monthly profit from the two stores was insufficient. I simply pointed out to Nelu that his complaint was with the Lord, not with me. He should take it up with Him.

It would have been easy, although unfair, to attach a degree of guilt to Nelu. For quite some time, however, I was tempted to do just that. Thankfully, the passage of time afforded me a fresher perspective as I tried to remain open to seeing things from God's viewpoint. Nelu had paid a great price in following Christ before the revolution. He had taken many risks. He also had a wife and family to consider. Along with this, the Lord had used Nelu to give birth to a new church coming out of the larger Nicolina mother church. This had been an excruciating delivery, as the mother church had had no desire to birth children. New churches did not mean Kingdom expansion; they meant Kingdom conflict; they meant competition. I asked Bogdan, Nelu's brother and original pastor of the new church, how the mother church had treated them. Bogdan responded that the FiloCalia leaders had felt "hunted" by the existing church hierarchy. This hunted theme would continually repeat in the future.

In the new church plant, there were many challenges faced in attaining recognition as a valid church. The old guard's ecclesiology was narrow in the extreme. All families and church leaders who became a part of the new church plant paid a price for their commitment and participation. Nelu himself had sacrificed much to see this new work started. He and a handful of other dedicated Christians dared to dream big dreams. They had trusted the Lord for great things for His glory. This was rare in those first days after the revolution.

Furthermore, Nelu was the driving force behind the governmental approval for the FiloCalia Foundation, under which the leaders envisioned a multi-faceted, vibrant ministry. This is primarily what had attracted Bob McCuistion to establish his ministry in Iasi. I was attracted to their boldness to try new things, to take risks. As I considered all of these things in Nelu's background, I had a clearer grasp of the situation in Iasi and I tried harder to understand rather than focusing on being understood. I wanted to be compassionate towards Nelu, someone who had experienced many difficulties that I had not. I was not, however, always successful in this.

It was challenging and at times discouraging to know that I was being obedient to the Lord's will but was not meeting the expectations of some of the key Romanians around me, like Nelu. It was a classic case of our financial resources colliding with differing cultural expectations. This was all the more acute when the divergent cultures had such a huge gap in economic wherewithal. Nevertheless, our association in ministry required us to labor together. My fragile position in this rapidly emerging partnership spawned many relational difficulties, misunderstandings, hurt feelings, and misconceptions of each other's agendas. We were attempting something new, something bold, and something fraught with cultural landmines. In time, I came to understand more of the troubling dynamic. God was teaching each of us as we learned from each other. I was learning a new language and how to improvise, making do with what was at hand. At this, the Romanians excelled. They taught me patience in getting things done; I was always in a rush. From the Romanians, I was learning to "let go and let God," something that did not come naturally to me. With warmth and grace, they tutored me in their customs and traditions, tactfully pointing out my mistakes and making exceptions for the new guy. Our store employees taught me how to handle client problems in a Romanian context in an effective manner. In our fellowship times together, they shared about their history, both secular and spiritual. I came to appreciate some of what it meant for them to be Christians under a Communist dictator. My new colleagues became my heroes.

For their part, my Romanian brothers were learning, among other things, punctuality. Their culture had a somewhat pliable relationship with time. I saw this as just being late. They were late to start church, late for meetings, and late for scheduled events. My Western background was rooted in the clock. A 9 a.m. appointment meant just that. We would schedule to meet at the FiloCalia offices at a given time. As was my custom, I would arrive a few minutes ahead of the appointed hour. I was always there first. Some thirty minutes later, others would begin arriving, expressing surprise that I had actually taken the appointed time seriously. Before long, they were discussing my punctuality among themselves. I must have appeared to them as somewhat of a clock Nazi. However, in response, they began to show up more and more at the agreed hour. We were growing in our appreciation and understanding of the unity we shared in our diversity.

The Lord intended all along that the business partnership would be what bound us together. It would be what anchored us in the storms ahead. At the time, I could only partially discern this. With hindsight, I can see it all very clearly. When we as sinners struggled with one another, our common, God-given vision was what brought us back together. The Lord, in His infinite wisdom, had provided in the creation of the business a way to impart dignity back to the Romanians. Thankfully, we were able to return to the bargaining table repeatedly. We Americans came with an idea and an ideal, while the Romanians had the shrewdness and pluck to pull it off. In short, we needed one another. This divinely appointed interdependency forced us all to depend on God.

And it worked. It worked in spite of us. It worked because God had ordained that it should work. Times without number, when there was conflict, we kept coming back to that original vision of partnership. It was this very essence of commerce, the quest for profit to benefit ministry, that the Lord used to unite and then reunite us. Returning to that point, we would then together pursue God's way forward. I wish I could contend that it was the Romanians who needed these lessons, but the truth was that I was learning in the same fiery crucible as my brothers.

Expansion

September 1993

Final preparations were under way at the new location for our second store, "Lilies of the Field." We rented the ground floor of an apartment near the west end of town, Pacurare. It would be a small store, modeled on the first one. We constructed a glass and metal wall in the second room, behind which we would do all of the sorting, ironing, and pricing of the goods each day. To announce our existence, in early September, we hand-stuffed hundreds of leaflets in mailboxes. After this blitz campaign, we were ready to open to the public.

For our new location, we hired additional personnel. Carmen had been an essential worker in the first store, so we moved her over to help ensure a smooth transition. I worked daily between both stores to accomplish whatever was necessary. There were still no other second-hand stores in the city, but that would soon change. I began to focus more on advertising and special promotions. Gloria, for her part, washed all of the clothes that came to us dirty. She had a rare combination of gifts: a steadfast servant's heart and a Kenmore washer and dryer at home. She would do load after load of laundry around her home-school lessons with the boys. Her contribution proved invaluable.

Clothes from America were still an anomaly in Iasi, so demand was great and our second location enjoyed a high volume of sales just like the first. Neither of our stores was a place that you would in any way remark upon if you happened to pass by. If you were a Westerner, that is. For our Romanian market, however, our stores meant the latest American styles and top-quality garments for reasonable prices. We trained our team (and the public) to recognize labels from Nordstrom's, Evan Piccone, Jonathan Martin, Ralph Lauren, and Hart, Schaffner & Marx. Profits from the sale of these garments, invested in ministry, were what we referred to as "business for mission."

Due to our accessible prices, I began to see a marked improvement in the manner of dress of the man or woman on the street. I could spot one of our garments in public, having myself opened thousands of clothing bags. I sometimes joked about the man who approached me begging for money while wearing a slightly used pair of Gucci loafers from FiloMarket. University students, professors, professionals, and the rank and file went about their Dacian day clad in clothes sold in our stores. Lilies opened to the same kind of mob scene we experienced the previous year with the original store. It provided twelve additional jobs for mostly jobless Christian women from a couple of different churches. The Lord greatly blessed our efforts. We had expanded our clothing network of donating churches in the USA the previous year. This provided us with the much-needed increase in volume of clothes on an ongoing basis. It provided something else as well: we immediately more than doubled our monthly profits.

The underlying vision, however, had nothing to do with clothes, sales, or profits. The Lord had created a Christian community touchpoint. Nearly 2,000 customers shopped our stores in a given week. Some came several times a week. Our procedure was to have new merchandise on the floor twice a day, so there was always something worth coming in to try on. The tranquil, relaxing atmosphere, enhanced by our Christian music, was a real draw. Beyond the ambience was the manner in which we treated people. They were free to browse, take their time, and return things if they were not just right. This was unheard of in Romania. Soon our salesgirls were developing friendships with store regulars. Of course, this interaction led to natural opportunities to share the gospel.

Most of our clientele were women; they began to open up to our staff about their struggles and problems. I encouraged our women managers to spend time with the customers. Each store had a tiny office so they could get one-on-one with people whenever the opportunity arose. On more than one occasion, we had customers who had never been to church come to Christ right in our stores. This aspect of our small enterprise was definitively business as mission. In this way, the Lord helped us to make the most of every clothing item and every opportunity.

After our first meeting in Berchtesgaden, Pastor Ronnie Stevens had become one of my mentors. He was unaware of much of his influence on me, but I received his throwaway lines as pearls of wisdom. I had been in

Romania long enough that the honeymoon was now over. There had been some real struggles and I was certain it would always be so. I remembered Ronnie's admonition to me before I launched: "Jeri, when the Romanians do things that make you want to slap them in the face, remember that you were sent there to serve them."

At the time Ronnie said those words to me, I recall thinking that there was no conceivable thing that Romanians could do to make me feel that way. I had come to see them as a warm, friendly, hospitable, and likable people. The Christians among them had truly paid a price for their faith. This was a price that I could not begin to completely grasp or comprehend, as I had grown up with democracy and religious freedom in America. I had great respect and admiration for the Romanian Christians with whom I co-labored.

However, these positive feelings did not tell the complete story. To introduce business, money, and profit into my relationship with my Romanian friends was to walk a cultural razor's edge on a daily basis. I had to face the fact that lurking in the Romanian pathology was an inscrutable tendency towards mistrust and putting the worst possible spin on any situation, real or imagined. For several years, I labored under the false notion that this was entirely due to fifty years of Communist rule. I have lived to outlive that misconception. This behavioral characteristic predated the rise of Communism by several generations at least. Because of this, part of the challenge of dealing honorably and effectively with my Romanian brothers was getting to grips with a kind of emotional blackmail they used from time to time. This meant that they attempted to put me on a guilt trip so I would do what they wanted. One of the times I experienced this was on the eve of opening another thrift store. I was doing this for a different ministry in the city of Suceava, some two hours' drive north of Iasi. Nelu Chitescu, our pastor, came to me, suggesting that through my time and effort in Suceava, I was "abandoning' FiloCalia. Thinly veiled in his accusation was the obvious perception on FiloCalia's part that I would only invest myself in projects that directly benefited them. I guardedly responded that the Lord had sent me to Romania as a blessing for the broader body of Christ. In my mind, this included, but was not limited to, the ministry of FiloCalia.

In the crucible

July 1994

Despite Nelu's efforts to dissuade me, in mid-July 1994, we were able to open a thrift store in Suceava with great excitement. I was on hand for the inauguration. I stayed with Costica Leonte, the pastor of a small house church there. We were creating the store for his congregation's benefit. Carmen joined us from Iasi for the final arrangements. The appointed day arrived and, as was the case in Iasi, the public came in droves. In some instances, they literally hurled the money across the counter for the goods they had chosen. It was another wall-to-wall zoo. Praise the Lord!

I had left most of the hiring up to Costica. All of the sales staff and the man he had chosen to be manager came from his church. There were seven employees, thus fulfilling a part of the original vision to create jobs for Christian workers. Furthermore, since there was no debt, the store was profitable from day one. It appeared that there was a brilliant economic future for this fledgling group of believers in Suceava. This was due to the Lord's wisdom in opening yet another second-hand clothing store. It was particularly fulfilling to be used in a small role to see the broader body of Christ blessed as we had in Iasi.

There are few things more satisfying than rest after long labor, especially when the Lord anoints the work. It had been a time of intense toil to see the Suceava project launched, as well as to put the wheels in motion for a third store in Iasi. So my family enthusiastically planned a three-week motor trip to England for vacation. On July 18, we packed up the car and headed off. Another grand family adventure awaited us on this glorious summer morning. We faced clear blue skies for the initial leg of what was to be a 3,000-mile sojourn.

However, our plans literally came to a screeching halt at the nine-mile point, just on the outskirts of a gypsy village named Letcani. Two little boys dashed across the road, one behind the other and immediately in front of our car. I slammed on the brakes and jerked the steering wheel hard left in a desperate effort to avoid both boys. It was to no avail; I hit the first boy with the residual momentum. His upper body arched over the front grill and his head smashed down on the hood. He catapulted forward, head over heels, some fifteen feet. He landed in the middle of the street on his side, his small body completely inert.

Inside the car at the moment of impact, I yelled at the horror of what was happening. My sudden braking sent books, tapes, and all manner of materials hurtling from the back of the car to the front windshield. The car came to a stop in the opposite lane. From there, I could see the young boy lying in the road ahead. I asked if Gloria and the boys were all right as I drove the car off to the right shoulder. I parked and got out of the car, telling my family to stay put. As I approached the figure in the road, I saw that he was a boy of about eight years old, wearing only a pair of shorts. As I knelt down to give aid, I noticed that he was still breathing and murmuring slightly. I picked him up in my arms and took him to the back seat of our car.

Life had taken on a surreal quality. Could this really be happening? By now, a small crowd had gathered around our car. I asked where we could find medical help. Someone indicated that there was a clinic back in the village. Someone else in the crowd had summoned the little boy's mother. Upon arriving, she saw her child lying on my back seat. She turned, and with flashing eyes, began to offer me the right and left fists of fellowship. At this point, I feared for the safety of my family. Things were turning ugly. I suggested that we needed to take the boy to a doctor. I implored the mother to get in my car so we could go right away. Understandably distraught, she agreed. We quickly made our way to a tiny house that served as a makeshift clinic, not 300 yards from where the accident had occurred.

I sat hunched over outside the clinic with Gloria and the boys. I was dazed, confused, and praying for the little boy's life. The fresh memory of the injured child caused me to ponder the sobering fact that it could have been Marcus or Trevor. My emotions were grappling with the reality that I had injured a young boy who, moments earlier, was enjoying the innocence of a summer's day. That was the beginning of repeated images that would haunt many a sleepless night for months to come.

Within minutes, the police arrived from Iasi. The markings on the patrol car indicated that they were the traffic accident investigation team. The boy was still unconscious and unresponsive. The village doctor arranged to transfer him to the hospital in Iasi. With my family, I followed the officers back to the scene in my car. Once there, the superior officer began gruffly barking questions and instructions at me. He told me to park the car where the accident had taken place. They measured skid marks, made notes on pads of paper, talked to those standing by, and kept up a stream of inquiries about what had transpired.

Clearly, the police were angry. An American with a foreign car had run down a little boy in a tiny village. In their place, I would be angry too. After an hour or so, they finished that part of the investigation. I had Gloria and the boys sit on the steps of a little market where I bought them soft drinks. I did not want them to hear the manner in which the police were treating me. I began to ponder how Marcus and Trevor would cope with all of this.[1] With the on-site investigation complete, the officers took us to the village police station, a converted two-room house. They interviewed witnesses while I sat outside. I was able to make a call and had someone come to take Gloria and the boys home. I kept them posted on what was happening.

The eyewitness accounts did not agree. The sketchy facts appeared inconclusive. The police did a technical inspection on my car to verify that everything was in working order. They finally escorted me to the police station in Copou, not 200 yards from where we lived. They took me into a room to give a verbal declaration, which they wrote down by hand on brown, unlined paper. News came during questioning regarding the boy's condition. The officer taking my statement had called the hospital to confirm the extent of his injuries, and the doctor gave the child's initial condition as "grave." This placed a far grimmer spin on the immediate proceedings. At that moment, I was unable to feel anything. The officer explained that everything depended on the results of a test to determine whether I was speeding. He asked for my driver's license. I remembered that I had not seen my license for months. I lamely suggested that it must be at home. The officer then pointedly informed me that I needed to return that day with my license or they would jail me immediately for driving illegally. At this new twist on things, I choked back panic. How would I tell Gloria? I was allowed to go home with the proviso that I return later that day to surrender my license.

Gloria took the news without emotion. She simply began searching the entire apartment to find the missing license. I was certain that it was not in our possession. I was racking my brain to remember where it was. Grasping at straws, I telephoned Nelu Moraru, our handyman, to ask him whether he had it. Perhaps he had inadvertently kept it since the last time the car was registered. Nelu assured me, however, that there was no way that he had my license. I told him what that would mean for my situation, and he promised to search his apartment. Nearly an hour later, our doorbell rang and Nelu came upstairs with a rather sheepish look on his face. He held out my license to me, meekly explaining that he had just forgotten to return it for the last several months. We averted one crisis at least. There was now a good chance that I would sleep at home that night.

I telephoned an attorney named Doina whom I had met when we first came to Iasi. She agreed to come to the house to discuss the case. Later, we walked back to the police station together. She told me to wait outside while she went in to verify that they would not assign one particular officer to my case. According to her, if a certain colonel handled my case, it would be a nightmare. I waited in the street. Some minutes later she emerged, reassuring me that she had taken care of everything.

I was to return to make a further declaration that day. As I sat at home until time to go, I reflected on the situation. The McCuistions were on furlough in the USA. It was summer, and many people had left Romania on holiday. We were alone there in Iasi. I telephoned Pastor Costica Leonte in Suceava to let him know the situation. He said that they would be praying for our family.

Later, when I entered the police station for the third time that day, they ushered me into the office of a Colonel Leica. He seemed reasonable enough. However, the intense interrogation that ensued was a stretch for my Romanian proficiency. It was, to say the least, disconcerting to have to communicate in an adopted tongue while under such duress. Praying for strength, I proceeded to play the hand the situation had dealt me. I was determined not to be intimidated or to let the colonel see me sweat.

There followed yet another dictated declaration. The colonel suggested that we could clear all of this up relatively quickly. It would, of course, be necessary to make some settlement with the family, based on the outcome of the investigation. He kept stressing that, even if NASA itself conducted the speed-test investigation, the results would be identical. He repeated this enough times to thoroughly convince me that he was lying about the speed test. He confiscated my California driver's license as well as passport. I tried not to let this "minor" fact disturb me but failed completely. I asked whether it would be possible to get my license back. The colonel responded that this would not be an insurmountable problem. He told me I could go home, but would need to be back the next morning. He assured me that it was just routine follow-up.

That afternoon and into the night, I tried to minister to my family. We prayed together. We prayed for the recovery of the little boy, whose name we had learned was Dorel Oncica. As an escape, we decided to watch all three parts of the Back to the Future trilogy. Gloria made a special dinner. We made the most of our situation. I was secretly praying that somehow we might be able to leave the country by Friday, as this was only Tuesday. That still allowed several days to work out a solution. That night, I went to bed and tried to sleep, but the attempt was futile. As with some gory film marathon, I kept replaying a video of the accident in my mind. This would go on for many days. The most troubling notion was that the little boy might not survive. The fact that I had injured a small child would continue to haunt me. Though not culpable, I felt horrible nonetheless.

The following morning my attorney informed me that Colonel Leica was in fact the officer she had attempted to shield me from. This was anything but welcome news. I decided to cooperate and be submissive. In the colonel's office later that morning, he gave me the news that the boy would suffer permanent injuries and that he was in a "grade three" coma. An additional declaration followed, handwritten of course, by Colonel Leica. How could I live with having permanently injured a child? I began to sense that this was going to take much more time and that there would be no quick fix.

I came home later that day to the news that the gypsy clan to whom the little boy belonged had come for me at our house. Our landlord's son-in-law, Romeo, had sent them away, telling them I was not at home. Romeo assured me that he would not let them through the iron front gate. He warned me that this group of a dozen or more gypsies had said that they knew where I worked and knew how to "get at me." This was just the little added wrinkle I needed in the fabric of our dilemma. Being the target of a police conspiracy was one thing; having my family threatened was unacceptable. I telephoned my colleague Tom Kepeler in Cluj. He agreed that I should send my family to him for safekeeping. I began to strategize the best way to spirit them out of the house and get them to Cluj.

In the meantime, we kept the boys in the house, as I did not want them wandering around outside where they might be potential targets. I really did not know what we were up against. We were now under a virtual kind of house arrest. The police were keeping us in the city, while the gypsies were keeping us within the walls of our home. At the police station the next day, they gave me the results of the investigation. The calculations indicated that I had been speeding, by about five miles an hour. There was no grace on this in Romania; not when an accident injury was involved. I had been certain that I was not speeding, but had no proof to my claim.

Back in the presence of Colonel Leica, I asked about getting my license returned. He became agitated, flailing his arms and saying that this case would now have to go to trial. A judge would render a verdict. With his outburst I realized that I was dealing with a liar. I made a telephone call from his office to Gloria; naturally, I spoke in English. The colonel bellowed at me that I was to speak only Romanian, so I did. After I hung up, he went on to say that the process could take up to a year, as the courts were jammed. He suggested that we talk to the gypsy family regarding a settlement. At this point I could do nothing but acquiesce.

The next morning, Nelu Moraru and my attorney Doina came to our house. It was obvious that they had been in intense discussion and were of the same mind about the issue. Doina laid out my predicament point by point. She informed me that Colonel Leica was waiting for a bribe. Without the payment of this bribe, my case would drag on with no recourse. The colonel was in complete control. Doina had brought Nelu to underline the necessity for this course of action. I asked Nelu to join me in the kitchen, leaving Gloria and Doina in the living room.

Once in the kitchen, I told Nelu that I could not pay a bribe. If I did, I would lose my Christian witness. Nelu pleaded, telling me that I would most certainly go to jail if I did not pay. He said it would not cost very much money and, besides, that was the way things worked here. Everybody did it. He finished by adding that only in this manner would the colonel free me from my deepening crisis. I thanked him for his friendship and concern, but said that, if I gave into this temptation, my coming to Romania would have been for nothing. I had to stay the course because God would judge how I responded in this trial. Nelu looked out the kitchen window to the beautiful sunshine flooding the garden below, and then responded forlornly, "You are right." We went back in to the living room and informed Doina of my decision. Stunned, she simply looked at me with her mouth agape, as if I had taken leave of my senses.

I now had a fuller comprehension of what my family was up against. I decided to call Bob McCuistion in the USA. It was good to hear Bob's voice as he began by assuring me that they were praying for our situation. I told him about Doina's visit and her proposal. I then said, "I really can't do that, can I, Bob? I need to stay the course, right?" Bob replied, "Absolutely, bubba. You gotta hang in there. You can't do what they want." With the police undoubtedly listening in, we still managed to communicate what was necessary in order to make a decision. Bob's words, although veiled, confirmed what my weak flesh was dreading. I would have to hold fast to my convictions regardless of the cost. Obedience was not getting any easier.

Some days later, I received a telephone call from my brother Jeff. In talking to him, I had to get across the fact that the police had bugged our telephone. I referred to the movie *The Conversation* that we had seen together years ago. Jeff got the message. He began asking leading questions and I did my best to answer in code. Earlier my brother had called Sam at CRM, demanding to know what the organization was doing to free me from this Romanian dilemma. Sam said there was nothing they could do and that I had known the risks when I signed on for the cruise. This did not go down well with Jeff. So I did not let my anguish show during our telephone conversation. I needed to protect him because he did not fully apprehend the concept of following God whatever circumstances arose.

That afternoon, I told Gloria that I needed some time alone, so I took a taxi out to a tiny lake just north of Iasi. It was a weekday, so I was the only one sitting on the grassy bank under a beautiful blue sky. I decided to go for a dip and dived into the two-meter deep water off the old wooden dock at the water's edge. I swam out to the middle and began lazily making my way back to shore, gliding on my back. Gazing up at the sky, the majesty of the clouds with the sun's rays glistening through them struck something deep within me. I began to pray to the Lord and thank Him for giving me such times as this. With my prayer came the realization that I needed to surrender my circumstances to the Lord just as I had surrendered my body to the water upon which I was floating. At that moment, complete peace enveloped me. God was giving me His peace; not as the world gives peace, but the "peace that transcends all understanding." This was uncharted water for me. The Lord revealed in that moment that I must abandon my will and trust solely in Him. Floating on my back in that lake, staring up at heaven, I told the Lord that if His path for me meant doing two years in a Romanian prison, then that was okay with me. I remember thinking that it would be fairly convenient since the prison was literally just a few feet from our house. Pastor Ronnie Stevens's words, spoken years earlier, now came back to me: "Where the Lord's will leads you, His grace will sustain you."

It was a revelation to me that the Lord had not brought me to Romania just to start new Christian enterprises. He brought me to Romania to bring me to the end of myself. Here I could not feign dependence on Him while covertly leaning on my own understanding. In short, I could not fix this. No amount of wheeling and dealing, ramming and jamming would make this go away. The Lord had allowed this to come into my life at a time when all of my usual support systems were not on hand. I had nowhere to turn except to Him. For the first time in my life, I experienced total surrender. It was electrifying.

The days that followed were a blur of increasingly rancorous encounters with Colonel Leica, efforts to monitor little Dorel's medical progress, and long stretches on the Nordic Track home-exerciser to release pent-up nervous energy. Handyman Nelu Moraru was taking foodstuffs to the boy and his family at the hospital almost daily. He had on three occasions taken food and money to their larger clan in the village.

One morning, the police called me to the office of a prosecutor along with Colonel Leica. Once there, the colonel told me to dictate yet another declaration. He bluntly ordered me to sign it. I demurred, saying that I would need to read it first. This really tested my Romanian. The document asserted that I had "caused" the accident. I protested sharply, insisting that I would sign nothing without my attorney present. Colonel Leica roared back that my attorney must come to the office and I sign the document within thirty minutes. I countered that my attorney, Doina, was on vacation for ten more days. Wide-eyed, the female prosecutor was stunned by the exchange and totally cowed by the good colonel, but I stood my ground. I could end up going to jail, but this pompous Philistine would not intimidate me. The colonel reluctantly yielded to my obduracy. Reduced to the role of a mere bystander, the prosecutor sat in disbelieving silence. We then broke and went to neutral corners.

Note

1 Much later, I was to learn how the Lord had been at work in Trevor's life even at that very moment of crisis. As instructed, Gloria and the boys had remained in the car. While Gloria watched with growing apprehension, she told the boys that they needed to pray. They were fervent, heartfelt prayers. Later, Trevor would tell us that, in that instant, God came alive for him and prayer became real. Truly, "in all things God works for the good of those who love him, who have been called according to his purpose," as Romans 8:28 tells us. I would not have chosen these circumstances, but they were God's vehicle for a ten-year-old boy to come face to face with faith. That day Gloria's and my faith also became Trevor's faith.

The battle rages on

August 1994

S
ummer lingered on. We were determined to make the most of our circumstances. We packed a picnic lunch and headed to nearby Lake Dorobanti to swim and escape the heat. The lake was crowded, but we managed to find a shady spot on the grassy bank. Gloria and I sunned and played cards while the boys frolicked in the water with all the other youngsters. Each boy would take turns running and jumping off the old slatted wood-and-metal dock. I kept up a casual watch on their movements.

It was again Marcus's turn, and he started from a bit farther back on the lakeshore for a longer run. As he gathered speed towards the now drenched and slippery dock, I nearly hollered to him to be careful. Reaching the wood slats, he took a last step at the dock's edge where wood was missing and it was bare metal. His left foot slid under the steel frame and stuck as his body cartwheeled forward, flopping into the water. His leg bent at an unnatural angle while his upper body was completely submerged.

I was on my feet and at a dead run towards the lake before conscious thought could catch up with what I had just witnessed. I arrived in time to reach down and take hold of Marcus's left arm, quickly raising him out of the water. I then gently dislodged his foot from under the steel gap that had entrapped him. Slightly dazed, I supported him as he stood balancing on his right leg. Calmly, I asked him if he could put any weight on his hurt left foot. He tried, but the pain was too great. I quickly carried him over to the lake bank, gingerly laying him on my towel. A crowd had gathered. I inspected the injury: there was a bluish-tinted gash across the top of his foot. We had averted tragedy, but I immediately knew that Marcus still needed medical attention.

My mind was racing, trying to decide what to do next. We had never needed any medical care since moving to Romania. I had always joked that prayer was our insurance provider. But this was no joke; having heard all of the horror stories about hospitals, I had steadfastly refused, until that moment, to consider them an option should a medical problem arise. The present circumstances were to test my somewhat cavalier attitude.

I glanced at Gloria and saw anxiety etched on her face. My heart sank. At that moment, a voice in excellent English, slightly tinged with a Romanian accent, caught my attention: "I am a doctor. May I be of assistance?" Instinctively I shifted position to make room for this man to examine Marcus. He was dressed in street clothes; everyone else had on only bathing suits. Bending down, the doctor deftly examined the limb. In a consoling voice and with a practiced air of professional confidence, he concluded that Marcus needed X-rays. He offered to drive us to the hospital to expedite the process. I thanked him and we quickly gathered our things as I carried Marcus to the doctor's car. On the way to the hospital, I reflected on what a coincidence it was that a doctor should be so near at the very moment he was required.

Outside the X-ray lab, the doctor spoke to the attending physician regarding the circumstances. Obviously, our new friend was a physician of some standing as we were immediately ushered into the radiology lab ahead of several other patients. An older physician, Dr. Pandele, would handle the case. They took the X-rays and discovered that Marcus had broken a bone in his foot and would need a cast. The doctor who had been so helpful bade us farewell. I thanked him profusely for his kindness, but he shrugged it off and said that he was happy to be of assistance. I never saw him again. To us he will always be a ministering angel the Lord sent at just the right moment.

In the wake of the car accident, Marcus's swimming mishap hit Gloria hard. Until then, she had maintained her composure admirably. Normally she handled times of struggle with a kind of sangfroid grace (helped by liberal doses of chocolate). There was something, however, about one of our boys sustaining an injury that momentarily took the wind out of her sails. This was difficult for her to process, as circumstances seemed to be piling one upon another. For me, as a husband and father, this only served to deepen my sense of helplessness. I was also growing increasingly exasperated with the police and their investigation of the car accident. Frankly, I was beginning to feel a bit sorry for myself. My attitude was focused on the fact that I could not "do my ministry" in the midst of all these trials. My perspective had become somewhat warped and self-absorbed.

I turned to the Bible for solace and strength, and again the Lord gave me the encouragement I needed. I read in Acts the account of the apostle Paul before Governor Felix. Paul was under house arrest for two whole years, during which time Felix routinely summoned him. Two whole years! The governor was hoping for a bribe from Paul, which would not be forthcoming. Paul had the spiritual maturity to discern that his circumstances were part of the Lord's will. It had not happened when God's back was turned; this was the Lord's preparation for Paul's next season of ministry. The Lord made it simple for me to see the direct parallel. Surely I could trust the Lord in the "light and momentary troubles" I was experiencing personally, in light of what Paul had endured. I came to see that this was my ministry for this time. I began to seek ways to serve within the confines of my God-ordained circumstances.

It had now been a month since the accident. August is the time when all of Europe takes a holiday, and Romania is no exception. My case seemed mired in a state of inertia, apathy, and the summer doldrums. Gloom was making a comeback. One day, I received a call from a mutual friend of Bob's and mine, a man named Cristi. Cristi said that he urgently needed to meet with me, but refused to divulge the reason why. I knew his reticence sprang from the fact that the police had tapped our telephone.

He arrived at our house some thirty minutes later. He began by explaining that someone in authority had become aware of my case and knew that the police were acting unjustly towards me. When I pressed him as to why anyone would want to come to my aid, Cristi said that this man had heard of the good works that I had been involved in for no personal gain. Apparently, the man was incensed that I had become the target of a conspiracy. He wanted to meet with me at my convenience. It was to be a public place somewhere in Iasi.

I felt no small amount of curiosity and incredulity. I accepted the invitation, arranging a lunch meeting the next day at the local Greek restaurant. Cristi was to accompany me according to the instructions. We arrived at the restaurant and the waiters seated us on the terrace where we took in the fine summer day. Cristi and I chatted stiffly while we awaited the arrival of the mystery man. I was dressed in a suit and tie, feeling out of place, but prepared for whatever direction the meeting might take. Finally, a well-dressed and distinguished-looking gentleman in his fifties approached our table. With practiced politeness, he extended his hand and introduced himself as Liviu Pangal. I motioned to the empty chair to my left and waved the waitress over to take our newly arrived guest's drink order.

We began to chat easily about a broad range of topics. Mr. Pangal spoke in a soft but steady voice, as his eyes scanned the other tables, taking note of his surroundings. We ordered lunch, the meal was served, and the plates were cleared. We discussed the weather, marriage, national politics, sports, and travel. I was enjoying the time, but wondered where all of this was leading. As the waiter served coffee, Mr. Pangal switched gears. He leaned forward after having surveyed the terrace once again. In a conspiratorial tone he began, "I have reviewed the file on your pending case and I must tell you that, in its present state, you will serve two years in prison." I listened, trying not to betray my alarm. Part of me wondered how he had gotten access to my police dossier. He was dressed, after all, in a business suit, not in a uniform.

What came next caught me off guard. He continued, "Mr. Jeri, Colonel Leica has falsified the facts of this case and has put pressure on the doctor to exaggerate the extent of the boy's injuries. He has also manipulated the findings to indicate that you were speeding." He paused for me to process the new information before proceeding. "It is essential that you now prepare a counter-argument to refute this falsehood with contradictory evidence." I asked him what he would recommend as a first step. He suggested that we begin with the evidence at hand and give a separate, private estimate of the speed of the car. Further, he indicated that we could start to document the proof that the boy would completely recover.

Cristi and Mr. Pangal began to discuss the particulars as I receded into the background. I felt like a spectator as they discussed the salient details of the proposed counterattack. Within minutes, Mr. Pangal bid us farewell, but not before assuring me that all would be well in time. His matter-of-fact air carried with it the unmistakable stamp of a man used to wielding authority. Who was this guy? It would not be long before I had the answer to this piece of the riddle.

I took a taxi back to the house. Cristi had agreed to meet me later after making a call at the hospital. After he arrived at my house and as we sat drinking mineral water in my living room, I asked, "Cristi, who was that guy?" Cristi responded that Mr. Pangal was the head of the Securitate for Iasi. He had held this position before the fall of Ceausescu. I had an immediate "out of the frying pan and into the fire" kind of mental flash. I asked Cristi what kind of payback this guy was going to want to extract in return for his services rendered, but Cristi assured me that he was not asking for money; he simply wanted to right a wrong. His feud with the police apparently predated my arrival in Iasi. Even so, I felt a visceral uneasiness.

The days that followed were a whirlwind of meetings and preparation of documents for our counter-charge. We asked the authorized specialist who was conducting the "second opinion" on the car's speed to get it done over a weekend. I paid a hefty premium for this, but judged it worth the expense to be finally on the offensive. Within two weeks, our case was ready. I was not present for any of the preliminary proceedings between Mr. Pangal, the police, and the prosecutor; I was not privy to the manner in which the machinations ground on during this frantic fortnight. All I know is that someone contacted me by telephone and told me to be ready on a certain morning. A plainclothes police officer picked me up and drove me to the prosecutor's office. The boy Dorel's parents were to meet us there. I began to feel as if I might escape the charges after all. Little Dorel had completely recovered and our second opinion showed that I had not, in fact, been speeding. The police calculation had not taken into consideration the weight of the car fully loaded. Now, if I could only come to an understanding with the parents ...

I waited in front of the multistory downtown building that served as the prosecutor's office. I admired its neo-classical European architectural style; the pitched tile roof and grand 19th-century ornamentation were very becoming. However, I was waiting outside the building, with my insides becoming more anxious by the minute. Finally, Dorel's mother showed up, alone and some thirty minutes late. She could not find her drunken husband. Inside the office, the prosecutor informed me that, while the father was inebriated, any declaration he signed would be useless anyway. He could come back later and easily refute what he had signed while under the influence. I was incensed! It would now be necessary to suffer yet another delay in the serpentine process of being set free.

Outside again, we found the father sprawled out under some bushes. He was beginning to regain consciousness after having passed out some time earlier. Next to his wife, he stood up on wobbly legs in front of me. She was short and he was shorter. I spoke directly into his bleary eyes when I told him that if he did not show up the next day at the appointed time, cold sober, I would see to it that he did not receive a penny of the settlement monies, even if it meant that I had to rot in jail. They both assured me that they would be on time and in shape. Not my finest hour in missions, but I had gotten my point across. I then went home, as there was nothing else to be done.

The next day, Mr. Pangal drove me to the same building and we waited in the car for Dorel's mother and father to arrive. On the dot, they came walking up to our car. Mr. Oncica had cleaned up well. Together we made our way to the entrance and climbed the stairs to the second floor, where the prosecutor awaited us. He reviewed the case and then he and the parents (with me somewhere in the middle) began haggling over money. A heated exchange broke out between the mother and the father. They were arguing in Romanian, but with heavy Roma accents (the language of the gypsies), so I could not understand a word. She slapped him; he threatened her. This went on for a couple of minutes. During this tawdry domestic farce, I peered out the office window, losing myself in the brilliance of that beautiful summer day. I felt strangely disconnected from the goings on. A wave of peace swept over me. I could feel only compassion and pity for this wretched family. At their worst, they reminded me of, well, me. My thoughts then drifted to Gloria and the boys, for whom at that moment I felt an overwhelming sense of gratitude to the Lord. They were all waiting at home to hear whether I was free or whether they would need to begin visiting me in prison.

My gaze and musings then returned to the proceedings at hand. The prosecutor shot me a look of chagrin and remorse for the melodrama the parents were staging in his chamber. I responded with a conciliatory smile. He was a pretty savvy guy. Surely, he knew this gambit was pure fabrication.

Once the prosecutor was able to restore order, we began to talk numbers. I offered a sum of money in Romanian lei. As if on cue, the couple erupted in feigned indignation at the paltry amount tendered; more money than they had ever seen at one time in their lives, and yet it was an insult. They quickly countered with a higher number. I paused, glancing at the prosecutor, who gave a slight nod. I had had quite enough of this farce. "A nod is as good as a wink to a blind horse," I reasoned. I nodded my acceptance of their demand. It was important, after all, that this family felt as if it had had its day in court and won. The session's haggling had cost me the equivalent of $500, but I was one step closer to sweet freedom.

The prosecutor's assistant counted the money and the parents signed for it. The father then signed the "hold harmless" agreement that had sat on the desk throughout the entire charade. His "wife" (it came out that they were never really married) helped him spell his last name, although still incorrectly. I thanked them both and expressed my relief and joy that their son Dorel had fully recovered.

As I entered the prosecutor's office the following morning, he handed me a stamped document with the heading "Neamurire Penala" (loosely: "Get out of jail free"), which I quickly signed. He then asked if all was in order. I replied that it would be once I had my passport and driver's license back. He said that I could go by the police station and get them that same day. We shook hands as I thanked him, and then I left his office. I was completely out of the building before what I was holding in my hand really sunk in.

Cristi was waiting for me in the street. He took the form and read the text. "Don't you want to shout for joy and go celebrate?" he asked in bewilderment at my subdued demeanor. "Maybe later," I suggested. I had the same feeling emotionally now that I had experienced physically at the finish line of the 1985 Long Beach marathon. I was at peace and yet totally spent and lost in introspection. God had shown me the bigger picture, and it was not about avoiding prison, pain, or personal loss; it was about trusting Him in all things; about having peace when faced with the prospect of prison, or whatever lurks when Satan takes a stroll. I kept turning over in my mind the object of another important lesson in missions, a lesson I learned on the mean (and potholed) streets of Iasi: one cannot long survive on borrowed passion. I saw that, in order to thrive on the mission field, you had to have a God-given vision and passion. The Lord had blessed me with both, and when combined with my feeble faith, they had given me the grace and strength to press on in the work that still lay ahead.

When I further meditated on this chapter in the life of my family, I was grateful that our convictions had been tested. We now knew the path we would choose even at great personal risk. God had been gracious even in my moments of weakness, which were many. In the crucible of circumstances, he had further purified my faith of some of its dross. I had grown and been stretched. As a family we were closer to God and to one another. I sensed that this was all somehow preparing us for the next phase of our life and ministry. Through this trial, God had been faithful, my family had bonded spiritually, and Trevor had embraced the true faith. For that last miracle alone, I would willingly have languished for two years in prison. After all, my sons were my primary mission field.

Our British brethren

On October 5, our third, "Gloria" store in Iasi opened to the quintessential mob scene. We celebrated that night at a local pizza place. During the party, the eldest FiloCalia elder, Donel Dascalu, rose to say a few words. He reminded the entire group that I had predicted that the Lord would open three thrift stores in Iasi in two years. He then pointed out that twenty-three months had passed; the Lord had fulfilled his promise one-month ahead of schedule! It was amazing to reflect on all He had accomplished in such a short time.

With the opening of the third store, I started to feel that perhaps I had finished my contribution in Iasi. I began to seek the Lord and His direction for our future. I was working a normal forty-hour week. This was pure vanilla to most of the world but anathema to the entrepreneurial fire that raged within me. I certainly could not hide behind what had already been accomplished and just coast along. I was certain that the Lord would not leave me to languish underutilized and underemployed at a less than frenetic pace.

I soon heard about another fellowship in the western Romanian city of Timisoara that wanted to open a thrift store. Mark Shipperlee, the head of a British charity, Link Romania, and one of the fellowship's donors, approached me about this. Link had become a clothing source for us in Iasi the previous year and our relationship had proven mutually fruitful. Mark proposed to provide the funds for the new store and to be its sole ongoing source of clothing from the UK. Sitting in my living room over tea, Mark told me flat out, "Jeri, we know you and we trust you. If you will work on this project, then we are in; if not, then we are not going to do it." It was nice not to feel pressured! I asked for a day or so to pray about it. During my time in prayer, the Lord clearly showed me that He was in this deal. I telephoned Mark to tell him that I was in. I knew that the Lord wanted what we had learned and been blessed with in Iasi to be shared with the broader body of Christ.

I traveled to Timisoara for the first time in the spring of 1995. It was a 420-mile drive from Iasi in our old VW Army van. I found my way to the apartment where we were to rendezvous. Cristi (not the Cristi who had helped me with the car accident, but a young man with whom Mark was working) joined Mark and me in Timisoara. Our plan was to walk the streets of the main shopping areas and get a feel of the city. This was as much of a feasibility study as we could do. Timisoara appeared more cosmopolitan and prosperous than Iasi. Amazingly, there was not yet a thrift store anywhere in town. The population was larger than in Iasi, and it was much closer to the border with Hungary.

We wandered down the outdoor mall area of the city center, window-shopping and meandering through several of the stores. At the end of the mall was a main street, across from which stood a beautifully ornate Orthodox cathedral. We dodged traffic to cross over to the front steps of the church. As we stood together on the steps, Cristi began to relate that these were the very steps where Securitate forces had gunned down many children after the revolution had broken out in the city. I could not help but be struck by the manner in which the Lord was bringing me full circle since I had visited Bucharest in the days following the revolution. The question on my heart then was, "How can I help these people now that freedom has come?" Now the Lord was showing me another facet of His answer. There would be a thrift store in Timisoara. The proceeds from this new venture would help fund ministry for a couple of different local churches.

I was to make additional forays into Timisoara, helping train their people and being on hand for the opening of the store. It was particularly fulfilling to see the Lord use Romanian, British, and American Christians laboring in harness to achieve His purposes. This store, too, was a success, and the clothes from England proved to be very much in demand.

In the fall of 1995, our lease was up on the original Iasi store space. It was just a small four-room house, but we concluded that we wanted to continue to operate our store there. The landlord was a Syrian medical student in his thirties. We arranged a meeting with him at the FiloCalia office to discuss the rent for the next year. He demanded more than we felt was warranted, then added that if we did not agree, he would simply rent the space to a Syrian colleague. We asked for a day to mull it over, during which time I suggested that I might be able to buy the space and thus eliminate the presence of large yearly rent increases. The specter of having to find new space and renovate loomed in my thinking. Approvals for commercial space were still difficult to obtain. Thankfully, the owner agreed to sell. His price was $25,000. I purchased the house with the help of C. J. List, another Christian businessman from the USA.

The deal went smoothly enough, and soon we were standing outside the notary's office with the Syrian to sign the final papers. Bogdan, one of FiloCalia's managers, informed me that he would have to tell the agent the amount that we paid for the house and then the appropriate sales taxes would need to be paid. The three of us stood facing one another as the Syrian suggested that we claim $500 as the price paid, thus needing to pay only a token sum in taxes. Bogdan readily nodded agreement and then turned to me for confirmation. I saw immediately that we had wandered into a situational ethics predicament. To agree would mean lying; it meant losing our witness to this Syrian unbeliever. More to the point, I would be reinforcing the false assumption (even among Christians) that you had to cheat to get ahead in business.

Instead of answering, I asked Bogdan to take a walk with me. In a whisper, I told him that we could not lie about the price paid. Bogdan countered with the sobering fact that to tell the truth meant paying $5,000 in additional taxes. With considerable animation, he leaned forward and said, "Do you know how much $5,000 is?" "Yes," I responded evenly, "today it's the price of our Christian witness." Bogdan simply stared back at me in bewilderment. We returned to where the Syrian, thoroughly puzzled, was waiting for us. Bogdan spoke up first and announced that we would claim the full purchase price. At this obvious lunacy, the Syrian just laughed. It was clear that he appreciated a good joke. But Bogdan assured him that we were, in fact, deadly serious. I added that I would pay the entire tax bill. As was customary, the token tax on a $500 purchase price would have been split between buyer and seller. I knew that the Syrian seller would never agree to split $5,000. He looked intently into my eyes, his mouth now agape, at the realization that I was indeed in earnest (and completely out of my mind). I explained that, as Christians, we answered to a higher authority and that we would not be honoring the Lord if we were party to cheating the government out of what was rightfully theirs. In response, I got a classic "deer in the headlight" look, followed by a slight nod of the head.

Bogdan then disappeared into the office to file for and pay the commensurate tax. This left me standing on the steps, contemplating how I would arrange to put up $5,000 more than I had bargained for. The Syrian and I chatted absently about cars and the relative merits of one make of vehicle versus another. Some fifteen minutes later, Bogdan returned to us with a rather stunned look on his face. I asked him how it went, and the Syrian and I listened as Bogdan related to us that the law had apparently just changed. Its effect was that the higher the amount that was claimed on a sale price, the lower the resulting tax liability. I asked how much was now due and then held my breath. "Only $600," Bogdan replied, slowly shaking his head in disbelief.

The entire scenario struck me as a cosmic set-up, a spiritual check from the Lord. If He could not trust me in the small things of the world, how could He trust me in the greater heavenly things to come? Who was my god when there was real money at stake? If I was truly committed to picking up my cross daily, then honesty was nonnegotiable. It has been said that our real character is who we are when no one is looking, and integrity is obedience to the unenforceable. Therefore, virtue for me must include accepting responsibility while leading by example and living in light of my faith.

Renewed commitments, new directions

Early 1995

Over time, it became apparent to us that no real change would come to Romania until there was a change in the prevailing mentality of the people. This would require instilling and modeling values that were more caught than taught. It would require shaping the next generation.

By this time, we employed some forty full-time Christian workers, most of whom would otherwise have been out of work. Our 1994 Iasi store profits were nearly $100,000, part of which were used to build the FiloCalia Foundation's building. (In the future, this facility would include Christian medical and dental clinics.) Our stores had also helped many in need, including numerous non-Christian young people. With store profits, we were able to fund Christian summer camps, where many of these young people came to Christ. These young, emerging leaders were then discipled, trained, and equipped for ministry. In addition to all of this, the stores were a good witness in the community because of the quality of goods we provided along with excellent service. As for me personally, however, I began to suspect that I was in the last stages of my involvement. On the business side, I had taken the leadership of FiloCalia as far as it was willing to go in terms of its vision. I felt confident that the Lord would give me a new mountain to climb, but only on His timetable. So I bided my time.

During their sabbatical, the McCuistions had taken stock of the first three years they had invested in Romania and sensed God calling them to further ministry in the country. Consequently, they made a move towards longer-term residency by settling into an old, ramshackle house and renovating it over the coming months. We were glad of their decision to stay, as we had also made a commitment to a second tour of duty. They shared with us that they felt called to focus their remaining years in Romania on the younger generation. This conviction was born of the many labors, with little result, to bring renewal to the over-thirty-five generation. They felt God's clear calling to pour their lives into a group of young, committed Christians upon whom they sensed God's anointing.

Jeff and Valerie Sutton, a gifted American missionary couple, had recently moved to Iasi from Germany and wanted Bob and Vicki to join them in evangelistic outreach to college students. Jeff had been instrumental in birthing a fledgling ministry to students in the dorms. A small Bible study group was meeting weekly. The McCuistions joined the Suttons in this work, bringing leadership and spiritual depth to the young Romanians who had a vision for college ministry.

At the FiloCalia Foundation, Bob had become increasingly frustrated with the lack of progress, vision, and unity among the leaders. The leadership was made up of good, well-intentioned men who unfortunately had become mired in the past and were unsure of the way forward. Bob saw much untapped potential in several of the younger men in the group. Over time, he sought out nearly a dozen young men, calling them to deeper discipleship. For the next seven years, this would be Bob's primary focus and consequently his greatest long-term contribution to the Romanian body of Christ. In subsequent years, these young men would form the core of a network that would reach many for Christ locally. They would also start their own missions movement, sending missionaries to countries such as the neighboring Republic of Moldova. This fellowship of believers became a church plant called "Ecclesia." In the initial stages, primarily students formed Ecclesia. However, as years passed, the group grew in maturity and depth, as well as in numbers.

Vicki developed a vibrant discipleship ministry to young women that complemented Bob's work of raising up godly leaders for the next generation. Bob had me take his place on the FiloCalia board of directors, given CRM's partnership in the stores and our long investment in their ministry. At about this same time, Gloria felt led by the Lord to take over the bulk of the home-schooling tasks for all our four children. This was an answer to prayer for Vicki, who was then free to focus on the discipleship ministry.

This, then, was the golden era for our three families. Once they had moved to Iasi, Jeff and Val Sutton seamlessly integrated into life in Romania. Their two boys, Matt and Chris, became instant best friends with Marcus and Trevor. For more than two years, we had prayed for our sons to have some guy buddies, so this was a huge blessing. All six kids got along famously, and we three couples were extremely close from the very beginning.

In June 1995, we sent our boys to the USA to visit family for several weeks. During the quietude of that lazy summer, I took extra time to be with the Lord, further seeking His guidance about our future. The Sriners, our landlords, had let us know that we would have to move from their house, as their daughter and son-in-law would need the space. It took me a while to come to grips with what a move would mean. I instructed Nelu Moraru to begin looking for a house for us to buy. During that spring, we had looked at one overpriced money pit after another. It was extremely discouraging.

Then, one day, Nelu came to me and said that he had found the house. In fact, there were two houses. He immediately took me to see them. They were located on a piece of property to the north of Iasi, on the road to the airport. On part of the land was a house already under construction. It had bare brick walls and dirt floors. The roof was only part-way completed. Next to this was a piece of land with a 150-year-old peasant hut. The parents of the man who owned the house under construction had been using the hut and the land. Now all of this was for sale. I took Gloria with me for a second look. We both thought it would be ideal for our family. Bob, as team leader, approved of our choice, and we instructed Nelu to make an offer on the property. We were able to agree on a deal and the papers were set in motion. We began to visit daily, making sketches of how we would finish the house and trying to estimate what it would cost. Each time we visited, I would cast a glance at the adjacent property as if to ask the Lord whether He would have us buy that for some future project. But the door seemed tightly shut on any such possibility. I actually felt relief at this, since finishing the house would be a huge undertaking for us by itself.

Experiencing God

July 1995

W e greatly enjoyed the deep fellowship that came with having a team. Together with Bob and Vicki, Gloria and I went through a Bible study course called *Experiencing God*. We met weekly and shared insights from this thought-provoking course and its workbook. As time went on, I discovered that the Lord was using this study as a compass to guide me to the next phase of our ministry. The course was all about watching where God was already at work and joining Him there.

One warm summer day, as I was praying through the *Experiencing God* workbook, I sensed that the Lord was revealing my future. He was leading me to an inescapable conviction. Gloria and I had considered for some time the possibility that the Lord wanted us to start a restaurant. However, the idea struck us both as so zany that we kept it to ourselves. Now, on the last page of the workbook, the final question was, "What is God leading you to do?" With my pen poised over the blank line, I hesitated. I knew that this would be a life-changing stroke. I could see now that all we had experienced in the past two years was a prelude to this moment. I asked for the Lord's confirmation as I wrote, "Build a restaurant in Iasi." I sat there staring at what I had just written. Who would believe me? What would our supporting churches and donors say? I felt mixed emotions tinged with dread and exhilaration. That was July 20, 1995.

It was a beautiful summer day, and I felt compelled to ride my mountain bike over to our new house, now being completed for us by Nelu and his crew. Upon arriving, I climbed up the makeshift wooden ladder to the second story and made my way out onto what would become a balcony. This overlooked the adjoining property where the peasant hut sat on nearly three-quarters of an acre. This is where we would build the restaurant. I stood on the open balcony and began to pray for strength and greater faith for the task ahead. I prayed that the Lord would claim this land and that we would reach many lives for Him through its use for His Kingdom.

On an impulse, I went over to the property, wriggling through the wire fence that separated what was now our land from that land. From the back of the property, where it sloped downward, I walked up onto a knoll that had a splendid vista over the city. "What a great place to build!" I reflected. From there, I made my way up to the hut. Wanting a better view of the land, I clambered up onto the roof and sat on the peak. Facing the terrain as it lay before me, I was completely mesmerized. I began to pray for revelation about all that the Lord would do in the future on this land.

However, instead of receiving divine illumination, doubt and fear assailed me. Nagging questions welled up in my mind. Apprehension filled my prayers when I considered how we would possibly accomplish everything. How could I explain my plan to all those who would take part in its completion if I did not totally understand it myself? Given my doubts, how would I respond in the face of the doubts of others? I implored God to give me a glimpse of what it would look like. I needed something to cling to with each step on the stony path that lay ahead.

As I sat alone on that roof, before my prayer was even finished, the Lord answered. I felt something like scales falling from my eyes and I saw the completed project. He would build the basic desired two-story structure with a terrace and then a garden beyond it. In an instant, the image vanished, but not the vision, nor the conviction. Those would remain to sustain me through long sleepless nights and the myriad trials that awaited me. CRM leader Pete McKenzie had taught me to "never doubt in the darkness what God has revealed in the light." Now I was bathed in the warm, affirming glow of that light, all doubt and fear vanished. At last, I had my new assignment.

I threw myself into creating a business plan. Our new house was still under construction as Gloria and I began thinking through possible menu items for the restaurant. We needed a theme around which we could rally to give coherence to the final product. I had already pictured an Wild-West type of structure, but this still left a lot of open territory. I remembered my time in Bucharest in December 1989, when I witnessed a phenomenon of sorts. The most popular television program in those early post-revolution days was Dallas. This was one of the first imports from the USA that had taken

Romania by storm. Every Romanian knew about Texas, Southfork, Stetson hats, and who shot J. R. Ewing.

I suggested to Gloria that we consider a Texas theme for the restaurant and feature our best effort at Tex-Mex cuisine. After all, we were true-blue Americans. This would make our little diner the only truly ethnic eatery in Iasi. We began making a list of possible names for the place. We considered "The Squat and Gobble," and then quickly rejected it. The next idea was "A Little Piece of Texas in Romania." Then I came up with "Little Texas East." We finally shortened this to "Little Texas." Our logo featured a cowboy in silhouette on a bucking horse against an oval background. We now had a solid framework for our beginning. I worked the entire month of August on a business plan. I read several books on starting a restaurant. I racked my brain to remember every lesson I learned working in restaurants some twenty years earlier. One thing was glaringly apparent— I knew just enough to be dangerous.

When I first broached the subject of a restaurant with Bob McCuistion, the idea hit him like a bucket of cold water. In time, however, he came to see the Lord in our vision. He and Vicki would be our staunchest allies. Without their willingness to take such a huge risk (on Bob's watch), we would have been stopped before we started. Bob was our team leader and his approval was therefore essential. Soon we were swapping ideas and recipes every time our two families got together. Having lived for four years in Iasi, the McCuistions were anxious for a quality eatery to become a reality in the town. When we went out to dinner, we never discussed "where?" There was only one decent restaurant in Iasi, an Italian wannabe that had opened a year earlier.

I began to immerse myself mentally in every aspect of the proposal. To come up with a concept was one thing. To bring it to successful fruition was a whole different ballgame. My doubt gave way to fear, and I could feel my fragile faith circling the drain. The question of how we would obtain and transport to Iasi all of the southwestern decor we would need to accent our restaurant was the key issue. I began to pray that the Lord would confirm to me in some way that He would provide the necessary items and the means to get them to us.

Later that day, Gloria was cleaning out a pile of bric-a-brac that had accumulated behind the clay oven (soba) in our bedroom. Things had been stuck there when we moved in and had sat collecting dust ever since. Among the flotsam was a cardboard tube, the kind used for safely transporting rolled-up pictures. Not recognizing it as ours, we opened one end and pulled out the contents. The tube contained a numbered lithograph of a famous Western painting called Bringing 'Em Home. We stared at the art in silence. I was trying to dredge up from my memory bank how this came to be there. It was a watercolor of a cowboy leading stray cattle along a trail. It was perfect for Little Texas. It was also something that we did not recall bringing with us from California. Later, it came to me that I had been awarded the lithograph during my years in the insurance business. I was convinced, however, that we did not bring the artwork with us to Iasi. I was further convinced that this was a quick answer to the direct prayer that I had uttered only hours before. Whatever the case, I no longer felt angst over the decor issue. I simply pressed on.

His ways are not my ways

Summer 1995–Summer 1996

In order to obtain the land next to our house, it would be necessary to negotiate with the parents of the owner from whom we had bought our land. Nelu made contact and the first inquiries regarding their willingness to sell. Apparently, they only used the land and hut for weekend visits and to grow their crops. But the property had been in the family for 150 years. Somehow, they had managed to keep it when so many lost their land during the Communist era. Nelu was a bit downcast after talking with the parents. He indicated that we could meet the couple on the land the next day, but he shared with me that dealing with the old man was going to be difficult. I was ready to show Nelu what a good negotiator I was, in part to compensate for my ineptitude as any kind of handyman around the house.

The next day, Nelu and I tramped across to their yard for a little chat. We sat outside around a wooden table and made introductions. The old man began talking about all that we could do with the land and its great inherent value. He was in the midst of a lengthy soliloquy, railing against the government, when Nelu caught my eye, as if to say that we were in for a long afternoon. The old man took a rare breath, and Nelu wasted no time in bringing up the subject of an asking price. The old man then said that he was not going to give away his land nearly as cheaply as his son had. He then named his price, fully 30 per cent more than I had paid for the adjacent land. He concluded by telling us that the price was not negotiable.

Nelu then turned to me for my brilliant comeback to the situation. I countered with the same price I had paid his son. The old man then launched into a spirited diatribe about how valuable the land was and that he was not even certain that he wanted to sell. The scene reminded me of the "negotiation" I had had with the Syrian medical student for the store property. So much for my finely honed skills as a dealmaker! I suggested that we needed to think about the price for a couple of days. We politely thanked the old man and his wife. After all, if we did not buy the land, then we were still destined to be neighbors. Nelu was as sure as I was that the old man was not bluffing on the price.

The next day in church I could not follow the sermon. I kept going to the Lord in prayer and asking the same question: "Lord, are you absolutely positive that I am to buy that land?" But the sense that the dye was cast remained intact. I was in fact to pay the old man's price. Later, we were back in their garden meeting their price and arranging to conclude the deal. I went home wondering if the old fox had not just hoodwinked me. Only time would tell.

In 1993, I had formed a company in Romania to use should I at any point need such an entity. It now made perfect sense to resurrect U.S.-Rom House Ltd. Little Texas would function under that name. With my attorney, we made changes to the original company statutes to allow for the various activities necessary for a restaurant. We completed this paperwork at about the time the deal closed on the land purchase. All was now set for us to embark on the project itself. We demolished the old peasant hut as a first step.

For the restaurant project, I estimated that we would need about $120,000. We already had $5,000 in cash for the project's genesis. I scheduled a fundraising trip to the USA armed with my sixteen-page business plan. I was off to the West with a Delta "Fly-Around" pass in my pocket and a God-given, bold dream in my briefcase. First I visited my friend Tom Sachs in Guntersville, Alabama. Over breakfast at a diner on the Tennessee River, Tom drew some basic building plans on the back of a napkin. That sketch eventually became Little Texas. I became a walking poster child for Little Texas. I spoke to people one-on-one, in small groups, in Sunday school classes, and as whole congregations. I poured out my heart over breakfasts, lunches, and dinners in homes and restaurants. But no doors seemed to be opening for me.

My last stop was in Milwaukee, Wisconsin. Through my colleague in Cluj, Tom Kepeler, I had contact there with Elmbrook Church, a mega-congregation of several thousand members. The church was a faithful clothing source for our stores in Iasi. Now I was ready to approach them with a new project. During my conversation with one of the key members, Glen Keddie, he said that it seemed to him that the project was too much Jeri and too little Jesus. He was for the idea, but was a bit concerned about how it would come about. His words caused me to stop and do some serious soul-searching regarding this new venture. Was it the Lord, or was it me? For the entire flight back to Romania, that most haunting and fundamental question churned repeatedly in my mind. I did a great deal of listening prayer on that return trip.

What the Lord showed me was that I was relying more on myself than on Him. I was striving to make things happen with my own strength, rather than depending on His strength. I belatedly came to grips with this rather wrenching revelation. On the one hand, I now felt a complete peace about the ultimate realization of Little Texas. On the other hand, the reality was that I had exactly $5,000 in the construction kitty to build what I had calculated would cost nearly $120,000. As usual, the Lord was simply waiting on me to align myself with His plan, His way. He was about to show me His perfect providence now that I truly trusted Him.

I soon received a message from C. J. List, a long-since-retired E. F. Hutton-broker-turned missionary. For C. J., I had coined the term "Romaniac." A Romaniac is a person with a surpassing passion (and exceedingly thick skin) for ministry in Romania. (C. J.'s tribe would increase over the years as the Lord recruited many more to His cause.) C. J. would travel each year to Romania and take part in all manner of projects throughout many parts of the country. At the moment, he was in Germany and had gotten wind (now how did that happen?) that I needed funds for a new project. Via email, he indicated that he had $30,000 in undesignated monies that he could commit to the project over the next several months. After my detour to enlightenment, I was finally on the Emmaus Road.

From the first dizzying days of the thrift stores in 1992, one employee had stood out as grasping the finer points of dealing with customers, merchandising, and marketing. Her name was Carmen and she quickly became my primary go-to person in running our three stores. I had put her in charge of the first store under my guidance. Now faced with the more complex and multi-faceted restaurant project, I knew that I needed a competent team to pull it off. I approached Carmen and offered her a position in management of our new vision. I had sensed her restlessness at the thrift stores. The FiloCalia Foundation, our partner in the stores, was not strong in developing people, so the brightest and the best tended to chomp at the bit and then leave for greener pastures. In the end, they agreed to let Carmen come work for me. She accepted my offer in late 1995.

With heaven-sent seed monies for the restaurant available from C. J. List, we bought mountains of bricks and tons of rebar in anticipation of the ground-breaking. This took place with the spring thaw on April 20, 1996. We had a little ceremony on the very spot where we would build. We were all present: the Littles, the McCuistions, the Suttons, and the Merrys (a couple who were with us that year for training worship leaders). Together we prayed for God's providence as I symbolically dug the first spadeful of earth. Soon we had a crew of some twelve workers, backhoes, and bulldozers, and nonstop, frenetic activity on the job site. I donned overalls and labored with the crew on most days. Additionally, I worked on emails and the telephone, endeavoring to raise the monies to keep the project going.

We had been in our new house nearly four months and the restaurant project was going smoothly. With a fence surrounding our yard and separating us from the construction site, I knew it was time to start searching for a family dog. The search became a family quest. Our foursome set about reading the newspapers for ads regarding canines for sale. We drove to one of the addresses indicated. Once there, we met an elderly woman who still had one brendle boxer puppy. The boys played with her a bit while we chatted with the owner. I knew we had found our puppy, but decided to wait another day. I wanted it to be a surprise.

On my own, I went back to get the dog. Cradling her with one arm, I drove straight to where the kids were having their home-school lessons. It was there that a certain twelve-year-old boy was about to experience a furry, four-pawed version of God's love and provision. Her name was Maxi.

During the summer of 1996, the work on our construction project was very physically demanding; we were asking our crew to labor at an unprecedented pace by Romanian standards. The work ethic in Romania had suffered greatly under Communism. We were paying good wages and feeding our workers daily, yet I was aware that I was asking far more than they were used to putting out. Consequently, I decided to try to motivate our crew by setting ambitious, but attainable, goals for a day or a week's labor. There was always the promise of a small cash bonus if they met the target goal. This they never failed to do, and I was constantly amazed at how much they could accomplish if I applied the proper stimulus. The initial monies available for building soon neared exhaustion, however. On several occasions, I excused myself from the work to climb the stairs to our bedroom/office at our house next door. Once there, I would pray for God's provision of further funds. Several times I was only a day away from needing to make payroll or a purchase of materials when we did not have enough money on hand. Each time, in some unforeseen manner, the Lord provided. I was always able to pay our workers in full and on time. The same was true for our vendors. Romanians informed me that this was virtually unheard of in their country. This made it all the more important to us, as Christians, since how we treated our crew, mostly non-Christians, would be a reflection of Christ.

One of our strategies to fund and build our restaurant was to have teams come from supporting churches in the USA on short-term mission trips. The idea was that they could come to help with the work and bring money that we could use to buy building materials. This idea received positive responses and we hosted our inaugural group in July from First Evangelical Church in Memphis. There were eight men and women on the team, all young people. We mixed and poured the concrete for the main outside staircase to what would lead to the upstairs. We employed metal buckets into which we would shovel the concrete, then we hoisted these, at seventy pounds each, up a makeshift fireman's ladder to fill in the fourteen stair steps. This turned into a fourteen-hour day of nonstop toil and sweat, as none of us wanted to call a halt until the entire staircase was completed. These men and women worked shoulder to shoulder and shovel to shovel with our Romanian crew. Such was the measure of the mettle of the dedicated folk who came to serve.

During that summer, we set a hospitality record that stands to this day. At one point, we had seventeen guests staying in our home. During this time, people began to appreciate more fully Gloria's gift of hospitality. Having so many people come to help with the construction meant also dealing with all their logistical issues. Meals, laundry, bedding, transportation, and communication became the grist of Gloria's daily grind. I never ceased to marvel at her organizational dexterity and energetic industry when applied to the care and feeding of our guests.

Nelu Moraru had been working for Bob and me since March 1993. He had given up a safe and secure factory job to do this. Some of his friends and family had felt that he was taking a great risk: the job might exist only as long as we stayed in Romania. Nevertheless, Nelu had seen it as a door to the future and was willing to take the gamble. Now, by the fourth month of building the restaurant, it was obvious that over-employment, not unemployment, was the far greater likelihood. Nelu brought everything he had learned on renovating Bob's house and finishing ours to bear on his work at Little Texas. The building industry in Iasi when we began construction in 1996 was not well developed. It was still necessary to travel to Hungary to buy many basic items. We purchased the heating system, wall outlets, fittings, conduit, and a host of other materials on long trips to Budapest. This made building something of long-lasting quality an even more arduous task. Nelu ran night and day to find all of the necessary materials, in addition to acting as foreman on the job site.

As the building neared the point of having the roof put on, Gloria approached me with an epiphany of sorts. She suggested that we raise the level of the attic and put in some bed and breakfast rooms to offer lodging in addition to the restaurant. My initial response was that I still had no idea how we would find the money to finish the project at hand, let alone take on anything else that would increase the finished cost. Gloria persisted, "You know that I have always said that I would like to run a bed and breakfast inn someday" (although I never remembered hearing her express such a desire before this time). She then finished with a classic, "You never listen to me!" My now long-term habits of eating three meals a day and sleeping indoors had become even more precious to me since marrying Gloria. Therefore, I felt obliged to heed her words. I simply told her in response that we would raise the roofline, but I did not want her to pressure me about finishing off any guestrooms in the near future. This seemed to assuage her tender feelings. Another bullet deftly dodged. I was fully convinced she would forget all about her idea and I would escape a future project. There was no way to know then how life and the Lord would conspire to chart our future expansion on the hotel side of the ledger. Later, it became clear that, although it had been Gloria's sweet voice speaking, it was actually the Lord's prophetic message.

Finishing touches

Spring 1997

We purchased much of our Little Texas equipment at auction in the USA. Working in collaboration with FiloCalia, Cosmo Tomaselli, our CRM staffer in Birmingham, Alabama, rallied church volunteers to load donated clothes for the thrift stores and all of our restaurant equipment into the same container. The ocean-going container finally arrived at the FiloCalia warehouse in Iasi.

For months, Gloria and I would discuss, haggle, and debate over how we wanted the interior design to look. Nelu, for his part, would then figure out how to pre-work the wood just so, in our very own woodworking shop. We went with a table-height wainscoting and solid-wood handrails for the staircase. We used a hunter-green shade of paint for the walls from the ceiling down to table level. This gave the room a warm and inviting ambience. Things were definitely taking shape. For a year, we had been searching out and gathering all manner of appropriate Western decor. Steve Hoke, at that time CRM's Director of Training, took it upon himself to contact Chambers of Commerce in a number of Texas cities. They graciously responded with several beautiful posters. We had all of these framed in our own wood shop. Someone donated several pairs of steer horns. Also donated were old horseshoes. Nelu had these painted black and fashioned them into coat racks. Over time, we managed to accumulate a plethora of Western art, pistols, statues, and other cowboy paraphernalia.

Our son Trevor had embraced the Christian faith as his own since the accident in the summer of 1994. Marcus had come to faith while we were still in the USA. Now, like Marcus, Trevor made time daily to be with the Lord and study the Bible. One typical noontime, he came to the lunch table. It was clear that something was on his mind as we munched on peanut butter and jelly sandwiches. Marcus was somewhere in town so it was just the three of us. Haltingly, Trevor began telling us what the Lord had been revealing to him in his prayer time. He believed that it was the Lord's will for him to spend a year of high school in the USA. At that revelation, Gloria and I exchanged furtive looks. Trevor confessed that he had been reluctant to tell us since it might then become a real possibility. The thought of leaving home was sobering to this thirteen-year-old. We encouraged him to tell us more.

I sat there in frozen amazement at the Lord's machinations. In the past weeks, I had also sensed that Trevor needed some time in the USA going to a regular school. I had quickly buried such thoughts, unwilling to consider splitting up my family. I was, I told myself, willing to go anywhere and do anything as the Lord led. My obedience was conditional, however: I would always insist that my whole family accompanied me. When Trevor finished sharing his heart, he looked expectantly at both of us. I was choking back my emotions and could not speak. Gloria then revealed that in her times with the Lord, she had sensed something similar. Now I was really choking.

Without knowing just what it would cost emotionally, I assured Trevor that we would be obedient to the Lord. I went on to say that we would begin praying about how we might arrange all of this.

Thus far, the Lord had provided everything we needed to see Little Texas become a reality. Another essential piece of the puzzle came together for us in March 1997 with the arrival of Jack Prater. Jack was a member of Pastor Bill Hay's church in Alabama and had owned a restaurant for a number of years. He agreed to come for nearly three weeks to help us in our kitchen with all of the necessary preparations. He took one look at the "hot station" that I had designed and asked us to leave him alone for a while. We all filed out of the kitchen in deference to his request. Some three hours later, Jack emerged with notepad in hand. He had managed to engineer conceptually how we would handle and deal with all of the kitchen orders once we were operational. Those three hours, in the hands of the Lord's "sent one," were the difference between order and chaos, success and failure.

Jack suggested that we do a "soft" opening to start. This consisted of organizing several consecutive evenings, by invitation only. We would serve each group and then have them fill out an evaluation form. Naturally, we invited the Christian community to help us with this gastronomic trial balloon. People were gracious to give us concrete criticism that significantly aided us in making needed improvements. The wait staff used this opportunity to learn how to coordinate orders and interact with the public. None of our wait staff had ever even been in a restaurant before. We were training these youngsters from ground zero.

Everyone was sad to see Jack go after he had had such an immense impact on our little diner. He had allowed the Lord to use him to create something new and unique in Iasi. Once back in Alabama, Jack kept in touch and continued to have an advisory role in our operation.

May 15 was to be our grand opening. Just ahead of this, however, I was the target of some heinous publicity. On May 10, the largest newspaper in Iasi, *Monitorul* ("The Monitor") ran a letter to the editor. In the main, the article pointedly asked the question, "Who is this Jeri Little?" Answering its own rhetorical inquiry, it went on to allege that I was the one who had for years brought disease-infested used clothing from Germany that caused illness in the children of Iasi. It further purported that I was now using my ill-gotten gains to open a new restaurant to enrich further my personal holdings. It concluded with, "I have heard of 'Tom and Jerry,' but who is this Jeri Little?" I read the misguided invective with a mixture of numbness and horror.

So much prayer, faith, blood, sweat, and toil had gone into getting ready to launch our little venture. Our ship was finally coming in. Were we now to run aground on the rocky shoals of yellow journalism before reaching our desired port of call? I tried to reassure our people that the Lord would protect us from even this enemy, since there was not a shred of truth in the indictment. I pondered what manner of written response would be appropriate. Then I remembered the old newspaper adage, "Never pick a fight with someone who buys ink by the barrel." I decided it was best not to respond to these spurious assertions. Later that day, however, I did move about town trying to divine some sense of reaction, outrage, or at least concern on the part of the public. I visited each of our three stores to encourage our employees. They had all read the offending article. There seemed to be no hint of a scandal brewing. It appeared as though the Lord had blinded the readers' eyes and given us His protection. I set the matter aside and pressed on.

Just ahead of our grand opening, the Lord conspired to bring us some welcome print publicity from a surprising source. A reporter, Radu Tiu, had assured me that I would have a very pleasant surprise when I read his paper on opening day. He was better than his word. The morning edition featured Little Texas in a full, front-page article. It was a glowing account of the inauguration of Little Texas, complete with several photographs. The headline read, "You no longer need a visa to visit Texas." It was something that my mother could have penned, so dripping was the article with lavish praise for what we had brought to the city. My first lesson learned regarding the media: the pen was mightier than the sword, and it was a double-edged sword at that.

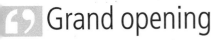 Grand opening

May 1997

O pening day was May 15, 1997. High noon was the appointed hour. How appropriate! We considered this a most propitious moment given that we were a Texas-theme eatery. A life-size cardboard cutout of John Wayne stood guard in our upstairs dining room, dubbed the "John Wayne Room" (what else?). We christened the downstairs dining room the "San Jacinto Room" in memory of where the treaty was signed between the USA and Mexico. Our walls were full of southwestern memorabilia depicting various facets of life in the Wild West. Someone had strung a ribbon across our railing as the forty curious invitees gathered for the little ceremony and awaited a few appropriate words from yours truly. There followed an official scissors' snip by the vice-president of the county board of Iasi. Then our first patrons filed in through the saloon-style swinging doors. Just at that moment, the music system malfunctioned and water began inexplicably to drip from the ceiling above the beverage counter near the entrance. "Now it begins," I sighed. Gloria had been working with her crew since dawn preparing what we thought were sufficient portions of everything on the menu. We had no idea what kind of volume to expect. Thankfully, our first day ended up being very encouraging. Magically, the music began working again after only a thirty-minute hiatus. The water leak stopped of its own accord. I spent the balance of the day running the front of the house with Carmen. I greeted customers, explained what a taco was, and made menu recommendations to our customers while they stared round at every inch of our place as if they were at Disneyland.

The days that followed were a blur, requiring me to wear many different hats, in addition to the Stetson. I washed dishes, worked the grill, cleared tables, and posed for photos with customers—we all ran nonstop trying to keep up. Gloria kept doubling the amount of food preparation each day. We would remain open in the evening until we ran out of the final portion of the last menu item. Customers would hurriedly compete to get at least something—it did not appear to matter what. "What do you have left?" a table of four would inquire. "Two orders of chili," followed by a "We'll take it." So it would go on. In a word, it was a zoo. There was major competition between the wait staff to reserve the remaining, lovingly prepared portions of Gloria's apple or lemon pies and chocolate cake for that day. Overnight, these delicacies became the stuff of dessert legend in our city.

This was the beginning of a dark cycle of missing time with my own family. Early each morning, Gloria made her way the thirty-two steps from our front door to the Little Texas kitchen. Late in the morning, I would saunter over to begin my shift. Inevitably, a telephone call from next door would interrupt even a short break at home for a few minutes. A customer had heard of our "wonderful new place" and wanted to meet the "Texan" in person. Donning my father's Stetson, I would be off to meet and greet some new patron. The upside was that this gave me a forum to share about the Lord with dozens of people from several different countries over the first few months. The downside was that I was steadily withering under the marathon pace. I would work until early the next morning when I closed the restaurant.

Arrival and departures

August 1997

June brought university graduation parties at Little Texas. The restaurant continued to be so packed that Carmen and I found ourselves splitting house duties. One night I would work in the kitchen trying my best to keep up with more than a dozen orders at a time. A given evening could mean up to 150 peckish patrons awaiting their Tex-Mex dinners. Carmen would work the front of the house. The next night we would switch. On and on it went.

We hired more personnel. We even brought Marcus on as a waiter. He would turn seventeen later that summer and I wanted him to grow up with a strong work ethic. Besides which, we were desperate for the help. This now meant that Gloria, Marcus, and I had a role to play, a place to go, and a task to accomplish. This, however, left Trevor at home alone. Our family unit was broken up for the first time. Gone were the pre-Little Texas family evenings together after a hard day at the thrift stores. In their place were nights filled with trying to hang on and get our restaurant crew to the point where they could handle more of the day-to-day. I was to discover that this was a process that would continue for more than three years.

The demands were taking a toll on all of our people. Exhausted and flirting with burnout, I began verbally to lash out at our employees for typical mistakes. I lost focus and failed to reserve venting my frustration for my times alone with the Lord. I was a poor leader and my crew followed my lead. In retrospect, the only upside to this was the opportunity I had to model humility when I would subsequently ask for forgiveness. This was something rarely displayed in Romania by leaders. Still, it would take a protracted period of time and trials before I would get a handle on submitting my frustration to the Lord.

With home school out for the summer, Marcus was free to work more hours at the restaurant. With him being the boss's son, I wanted to make sure he got no special treatment. Carmen typically gave him the worst tables and shifts. This left more of the gravy for those who needed to make a living with us.

Mercifully, with the coming of August, much of Iasi had left on vacation and things slowed a bit. We also closed for three weeks, giving everyone a much-needed break. I gave the entire Little Texas crew the time off. This was more to give everyone a rest than to conform to any preconceived strategy on our part.

As a family, we took a vacation in Western Europe, stopping in Budapest on our way back to Romania. This was a good time for the whole family to rest and reconnect with one another. It was also now time to face the stark reality of our decision to send Trevor to the USA for a year of high school in California. Marcus would also be leaving us temporarily to travel to Russia. He had received an invitation to visit some of CRM's staff in St Petersburg for ten days. He had worked hard all summer at Little Texas and had saved up his own money. We agreed to let him go; he was, after all, nearly seventeen. He was to fly from Budapest the same day that Trevor would fly on to California. Trevor would live with Gloria's sister and brother-in-law and go to school in California for his ninth-grade year.

We drove out to the Budapest airport that morning. Once their bags had been checked, we waited for the boys' flights. We were dreading the goodbyes yet to be said. Marcus left for his gate first. We then hugged Trevor and watched him walk through security.

As we traveled back home, we were only about ninety minutes' drive from home when a lone policeman pulled me over in the town of Piatra Neamt. The streets were deserted, as it was nearly midnight. I knew that I was not speeding, so wearily, but unconcerned, I climbed out of the car, more than a bit perplexed. The paunchy, middle-aged officer was standing in the middle of the street and asked for my papers. I dutifully handed them over, asking him why he had stopped me. He did not respond. Stone-faced, he silently scrutinized my license and registration. After fully two minutes of scrutiny, during which time I began to feel the full weight of road food and fatigue, the officer announced that my papers were not in order. Looking me straight in the eye, he dramatically thrust them behind him, straightened his back, and stuck out his lower lip for added emphasis. I was initially inclined to succumb to his antics. After a time, however, the thought occurred to me that this was just another attempted swindle. I was determined that it would be the last. Glancing up and down the street, I quickly verified that we were in fact alone. Standing nose to nose with this uniformed miscreant, I asked if he was carrying a gun. Somewhat puzzled, he answered that he was not. "In that case," I told him, "I will just take my papers and go home." I quickly reached behind his back and snatched the documents, turned on my heels, and sped away in the car. I glanced back in the rearview mirror in time to see him standing with his mouth agape, incredulous at what had just transpired. Interestingly enough, from that time on, we were never again the target of such harassment.

At last we reached Iasi, physically and emotionally drained from the day's arrivals and departures.

We lost no time in recapturing our daily rhythm. Back in the saddle, I began taking a closer look at the numbers and the accounting. It was necessary to invest more of my personal money to bring some of our inventories up to par. This was due to being closed three weeks with no revenue coming in. However, I was not entirely convinced that there were not other, more sinister factors at work. No matter how much money came in the front door, it seemed that we had great difficulty keeping enough funds to maintain all aspects of our operation. We had contributed to ministry in late June and at the end of July. I knew that I would lose heart if we were not at least giving some monies to ministry early on. I had targeted a 10 per cent net profit level for the restaurant. This was a dart-board approach, not the least bit strategic. I figured that 10 per cent was the basic tithe called for in Scripture, so it seemed right to have this as an initial target for Little Texas.

September was a busy month at Little Texas. However, at month end, we did not have enough cash on hand to pay the monthly taxes. This seemed ludicrous to me. I knew that we had a shrinkage problem (diner-speak for "theft"), but I was beginning to see that if I did not take the bull by the horns, we would probably go under.

Elsewhere, the ministry that Bob and Vicki had put their hands to was thriving. The Ecclesia Church was growing, young people were coming to

Christ, new leaders were emerging, and the ministry was multiplying. The restaurant and our thrift stores helped to support financially this vibrant evangelistic work. The Suttons and the McCuistions were extremely supportive of Little Texas, but Gloria and I were alone as far as the day-to-day running of the place was concerned. I knew that I had to get my arms around the big picture.

For some time, I had been feeling the ill effects of working too hard under constant stress. I was pressing on in my own strength, a fundamental error for any Christian. I was miserable, but so wanting to be made whole again, to get the joy back. Misery must in fact love company, as I was doing a stellar job at making everyone around me miserable as well. Gloria reached out and stood by me. It was tough on her. She ended up getting far more than she bargained for in starting a restaurant. Somewhere deep inside, I was aware that God was still in control. He had allowed these circumstances to come into my life. They were His best for my ultimate good. Jeremiah 29:11 and Romans 8:28 spoke so eloquently of this fact. This did not mean, however, that living through the process would be easy. The question I began to ask myself was whether I was disqualifying myself from ministry. We had for more than a year planned to travel back to the USA for several months, starting in May 1998. Would our return there be the end of it all?

The Lord graciously allowed Little Texas to turn the corner in October. FiloCalia received its percentage of profit and we supported the Ecclesia ministry by helping to pay the rent at the "House of Books" (where the church currently met for Sunday evening services and mid-week Bible studies). I felt extremely fulfilled, knowing that we had managed to keep to the original vision of Little Texas supporting local ministry.

Christmas 1997 gave us a much-needed break when we closed for four days. We flew Trevor home for his Christmas vacation. It was so heartwarming to spend time together as a whole family, even if only for a few days.

The Way of Joy

1998

In early 1998, one Sunday at church, a new ministry came to my and Gloria's attention. I was familiar with Valentin Chirica as a member of our church, but had not really gotten to know him. That Sunday morning, he went up to the front during the time of sharing and spoke of how the Lord had put it on his heart to minister to the poorest of the poor in Iasi. Valentin visited little children whose parents had abandoned them in the hospital, and was also working with youngsters through a children's club he had started. There was something winsome in the glow of his countenance as he asked for prayer for his ministry. I leaned over to Gloria and whispered that we needed to get to know this man.

We began supporting Valentin and his work with a very tiny sum of money per month to provide for fruit and chocolate for the little ones he would visit at the hospital. I once accompanied Valentin on his visit to the children's hospital that was just up the street from our first thrift store. The children's response to Valentin's presence when he entered their hospital room mesmerized me. He was father, mother, and big brother all rolled into one. Several cherubs shouted his name and reached for his embrace from their crib beds. One darling little girl, age three, had been abandoned for a full year. She was in need of a throat operation. Valentin explained that she would chew the chocolate with great relish, but then had to spit it out, as she could not swallow. Staggered by such suffering, I lost it at that point and had to go out into the hall.

Valentin told them about Jesus and His love for them. He promised to come back soon with more treats. I promised myself that we would continue to support Valentin and the heartwarming work that he was doing. I marveled at such people whom God called to minister among the forgotten and cast aside among us. Over the next several years, we would take every step with Valentin as his ministry grew and expanded into Calea Bucuriei (The Way of Joy, or WOJ). In time, we helped to provide the funding for a location where the ministry could have expression. The upstairs-downstairs location was ideal as it was within easy walking distance from a large apartment block, abandoned by the city leaders. There in the Phantom block (renamed Jeremiah) some 110 families lived in abject, grinding poverty. The block had no heat, running water, or plumbing. Originally, we paid to have the water from our nearby space be made available so that the families could come and carry water back to their tiny flats. They came to the WOJ with buckets, pails, canisters, and bottles. They took back with them water to cook, water to clean, water to live. They knew it as "the living water" because there they also found Jesus.

Valentin and I separately, but in complete unity, felt the Lord calling us to see a church started among these people. No such church existed to specifically reach out to the poor. They were not welcome in other churches. They smelled, they were unwashed, and, mostly, they were unwanted. However, they too were the Lord's creation and He would offer salvation to them, even to them. At first, Valentin began Bible studies for the men and women, in addition to a daily kindergarten and afternoon kids' clubs. Valentin was not only a kind of "Father Theresa," he was also somewhat of a Pied Piper. He was a human magnet for caring and dedicated volunteers to the ministry. Luminita and Mihalea, two young Romanian women in their early twenties, began to work with the children and develop the kindergarten and afternoon clubs. More than 120 children would come each week. Regular schools would not accept these youngsters and the parents had no money to send them to private kindergarten, of which there were many in Iasi. During the morning program, the staff fed each child a sandwich and some fruit. For many, this was the only food they had to eat all day. So began a more holistic approach to sharing the gospel. We endeavored to meet very basic human needs while sharing the love of Jesus right where these people lived.

With the help of First Evangelical Church in Memphis, we managed to renovate the entire space, building a kitchen in the second downstairs room and a shower facility in the tiny courtyard. Thus, we introduced hygiene where people sorely needed it. Valentin's staff oversaw the shower program. There were days for the girls and days for the boys. One mother took her four-year-old girl into one of the two pristine stalls where together they enjoyed a hot shower. This was the first shower in the little girl's life.

When finished, the mom told the little girl that it was time to go. The little girl then pleaded, "Mommy, can't we just live here now?" The following Sunday, we saw the official birthing of the Way of Joy Church. Many came to Christ and began growing in their faith. The vision had come full circle.

In my first meeting in January 1998 with Carmen, I could sense a change in her attitude. She had so many times held me up and kept me going during the past year, but now I noted a shift in her focus. She was beginning to press me about her future earnings and what was in it for her. I explained that we were still working to get things on a more solid footing profit-wise. She had worked extremely hard and had sacrificed much; however, I felt as if I was fairly compensating her. But she was now making a case for a percentage of the profit as a part of her pay package. I tried to explain that "cash on hand" was not profit, since we would soon spend it on basic daily materials. She did not seem satisfied, but dropped the matter all the same. As manager, Carmen was making more than twice what I paid other employees. I intended to sweeten this as we attained a greater degree of profitability.

Later, I heard a rumor. Rumors, often false or, at the very least, inaccurate, were always rife in our situation. Carmen allegedly was insisting that I had promised her certain things and had not delivered. Now she would "get back at me" for not keeping my word.

Concerned and baffled, I sat down with Carmen and repeated to her what I had heard. She laughed aloud at the very suggestion. She did it in such a way as to convince me of the rumor's truth. I attempted to reassure her that she was a big part of our future, but told her that, as in the first year of almost any start-up business, there was not yet enough profit with which to further compensate key people. I then reminded her of the $4,000 gift we had given her to finish her house. I was disappointed to observe that this seemed to make no difference at all.

Carmen had made a connection with a Turkish bank president who frequented Little Texas for dinner during his business trips to Iasi. In time, she asked for a couple of days off to go to Bucharest and develop this business relationship. Of course I let her go, as it was good to have someone besides me actively engaged in customer relations. Feelings that something was amiss still nagged me, however. Nevertheless, I could not put my finger on just what. Living way behind the information curve was just a way of life for an American in Iasi. Especially this American.

In May 1998, on the eve of our departure for several months in the USA, we organized an employee party. We invited each person's family, and everyone enjoyed the sunshine on our restaurant terrace. Earlier we had purchased a ping-pong table, a big hit at the picnic. Seeing the spouses and children of our employees playing together filled me with a keen sense of just how many lives Little Texas was impacting.

Cosmo and Susette Tomaselli, a CRM staff couple, had come to Iasi for the summer. They would be staying in our home to help oversee things during our absence. I was leaving Carmen nominally in charge of daily operations. This strategy theoretically afforded us the freedom to be gone for an extended period without things falling apart. It was a fine plan, as far as theories go. In practice, it would prove to be an unmitigated disaster.

The first month of our US visit was full of reconnecting with family. CRM, concerned about my exhausted state, insisted that I not do any speaking or other forms of "work." This proved to be a wise interdiction. I was spent, physically and emotionally. Family and friends of our ministry were extremely gracious to offer us their vacation places to enjoy. Gloria and I stayed with my sister Jill part of the time we were in California. I kept in contact with Little Texas through email and regular telephone calls.

We spent Independence Day at the home of friends from our church, thoroughly enjoying the fellowship and being in the USA for this most American holiday. My thoughts were about how the July 4th celebration at Little Texas was going. I had given Carmen strict instructions and parameters as to what she could do and how much she could spend. The next day I received a telephone call from Bob McCuistion. I sat alone on the bed in the guestroom listening in stunned silence to what Bob very reluctantly reported to me. The Little Texas July 4th event, it would appear, had not gone well. More than 200 customers attended and it seemed that they had roundly enjoyed the evening's entertainment. The problem was that Carmen had spent us into the ground. She had hired a known band and paid for their travel and lodging in Iasi. In addition, she admitted many people to the event who did not pay. Furthermore, she had made extravagant promises to our crew that she would give them big bonuses from the monies earned off the event. This money had not materialized.

In the days that followed, it became more apparent just how much we were in the hole from Carmen's spending spree. Though 7,000 miles away, I was responsible. Cosmo had the worst of it because, for the entire run-up to the event, Carmen had kept him in the dark. Not speaking the language, he was no match for her.

Bob went on to reveal yet another situation that had come to his knowledge. In the restaurant office in our home, handyman Nelu Moraru had inadvertently come across a document showing that the ownership of Little Texas had recently been changed. With great reluctance, Nelu approached Bob with the document. According to the paperwork, Carmen was now the majority owner of Little Texas. Clearly, something was awry. Bob decided to speak to Carmen regarding this to get her side of the issue. Carmen feigned surprise and even amusement that anyone could make such a "mistake." She assured Bob that our escrow agent, Mrs. Frost, must have done it quite accidentally. Bob decided to accept Carmen's explanation for the time being, given all of the other problems from the July 4th fallout.

Later that day, I telephoned Carmen in Iasi. When I asked her about the ownership document, she quickly dismissed it as a misunderstanding. I wanted to take her at her word, so I dropped the subject. Before hanging up, I reiterated my conviction that Little Texas existed to bring glory and honor to God. It did not belong to me or to anyone else.

The main event of our vacation in the USA was to be a cross-country road trip with Gloria and the boys. One of our first stops was a visit with friends, the Merrys, in Arizona. While Gloria was sleeping, I squirreled myself away to speak privately to Bob. I ended up listening for more than thirty solid minutes as Bob filled me in on the latest sordid news. Evidently, he had discovered much more in the past couple of days.

He began by telling me that he had been inclined to accept Carmen's explanation of how the incriminating ownership documents had come into existence. Upon further digging, however, it was determined that there was no way that our notary, Mrs. Frost, could have drafted such a document without specific instructions from someone. Again Bob confronted Carmen. This time Carmen's husband, Daniel, was present, along with Vicki and Cosmo. The dreaded and agonizing meeting took place in our living room. Cornered and opposed by the staggering weight of irrefutable evidence, Carmen finally conceded the truth. She had willfully redrawn the papers, giving herself controlling interest. She had also spent us into several thousand dollars of debt from the July 4th event. Unfortunately for Carmen and her wellbeing, she was very sorry that she had been caught, but there was no genuine repentance.

Furthermore, under her poor leadership, employees felt that they could come and go and do as they pleased. We were now dealing with a form of anarchy at Little Texas. Although we would never know if there actually was any outright theft of monies, the theft of foodstuffs was rampant.

Carmen's husband, Daniel, realizing now for the first time what she had done, boldly stated that Carmen could no longer work for Little Texas. Bob had hoped that she herself would offer to resign. In any case, Bob was determined that Carmen, from that day on, would no longer have any connection to Little Texas. Daniel was a good man with a tender heart. His reaction to these startling revelations regarding his wife was a mixture of shock and shame. His decision as spiritual head of his household that Carmen would have to quit saved the situation as well as the need for an uncomfortable dismissal.

I had been listening in mummified silence. Bob finished his overview with a weary, slow exhalation. I grasped the receiver more tightly. It was obvious that he had been through hell in the past few days. I wondered if we would ever come back from this fall from grace. One of our founding principles for doing business in Romania was not to involve the other vocational staff directly in the business. Now it had been necessary for Bob and Vicki to wing in to save the day. This took untold man-hours and a great deal more emotional energy. Here again, I was staring in the face of failure on the mission field.

I assured Bob that I would do whatever it took and agree to any decisions he made. I was, after all, under his authority. With far more conviction than I felt, I offered to return immediately to Iasi. Bob counseled me that it was best to continue our furlough as planned. Bob had anticipated my question as to who would run things for the time being. To my great relief, he had already approached Jeff Sutton about taking over for Cosmo, and he was agreeable. Jeff was willing to serve in my stead because he believed in the vision of Little Texas. Bob was confident, as was I, that with Jeff at the helm, things would improve. I thanked Bob for his essential help in such a delicate and thorny situation. Nevertheless, I hung up the telephone feeling that there was no real future for the Little Texas vision in Iasi. I joined my family at the dinner table with the Merrys, feeling anything but merry.

Betrayal

Summer 1998

O ur son Marcus had now graduated high school, through our home-school curriculum in Iasi. He would now remain in the USA to begin his university studies that fall of 1998. In August, we decided that I would return to Iasi for one month, ahead of Gloria. This was at the same time that Marcus turned eighteen and was therefore eligible to obtain a driver's license without the formalities of schooling. For Gloria, it was somewhat of a nerve-wracking experience to hand Marcus the keys to a used Chevrolet, literally the day after he got his license, wish him well, and then get on a plane for Romania. This tended to improve the parental prayer life while still tearing at the hearts of a mom and dad.

Now that we had Marcus settled in and attending university in California, we returned to Iasi. My passion to help fund such ministries as Ecclesia and the Way of Joy burned in me as deeply as ever.

Once back, I made a point of meeting with Carmen. There was a total lack of remorse on her part. Clearly, she had been seduced by the dark side. She had sought the applause of men over the pleasure of the Lord. Being in the orbit of people with power and wealth had blinded her. It reminded me of the telling admonition from Proverbs 23:1–2:

When you sit to dine with a ruler,
note well what is before you,
and put a knife to your throat
if you are given to gluttony.

With Carmen gone from the staff, Jeff Sutton had promoted Maria Moraru, Nelu's wife, to manager in another important move. So now, in addition to Nelu building and maintaining Little Texas, his wife Maria went from part-time bookkeeper to manager. I now dived into a daily role alongside Maria.

At this time, I revisited Gloria's original suggestion that we convert the large floor space above the restaurant into a bed and breakfast for travelers to Iasi. Work was begun by Nelu and his crew upstairs, while Maria and I concentrated on expanding our customer base downstairs in the restaurant. The fact that there was still no decent eatery in Iasi besides Little Texas greatly aided us. The wave of competition would come soon enough, of that I was sure. So in addition to increasing restaurant revenue, I was determined to finish the four bed and breakfast rooms above the restaurant. This was by way of keeping a promise to Gloria, in addition to seeing the rooms as a second profit center.

The Lord provided for our new rooms in quite an unexpected way. Nathan, a young volunteer from Birmingham, Alabama, had come to help build Little Texas in summer 1997. He put us in contact with his boss, Tom Vignuelle. Tom was the son of the senior pastor for SMI church, which had supported us for years. Tom owned a bed factory and a showroom in the Birmingham area. Over the telephone, I quickly shared my need to buy some quality beds. Actually, it was a bit of a bluff. In fact, I had no money for beds, but I needed them, and it was time to make arrangements. Soon we were to have all of the furnishings shipped over on a container of clothes from Birmingham.

The next thing I knew, Cosmo, back again in the USA after his and Susette's summer in Iasi, emailed me to say that the beds had been delivered to our mini-storage in Birmingham. There was no amount due on the bill; Tom had donated all six custom-made beds for Little Texas. Of course, I wrote and thanked him profusely for his generosity, totally unaware of how this gift had come about. I would hear that story on my next trip to Birmingham. In the meantime, thanks to Cosmo and Susette, we had yet another container of clothing for our three stores, plus all of the furnishings for the mini-hotel rooms, steaming towards Romania. Most of the final costs for the rooms we took out of restaurant revenue. The space above the restaurant was really taking shape. Each room would have a large cable television, luxurious carpet, plush towels hanging in a spotless bathroom, upholstered wing-back chairs, and a fully stocked mini-refrigerator.

Nowhere in our entire region of Romania was there a comfortable hotel bed. For that, you had to go to Bucharest, a good six hours' drive to the south. Little Texas changed all that. We actually had an Israeli businessman come to us four days ahead of our scheduled opening. Fortunately for us, thousands followed his lead.

Thus we had taken our first step in developing what would become much more of a hotel destination in the future. To my bemusement, the rooms were far more profitable than the restaurant on a percentage basis. For all my so-called business acumen, the Lord had handed Gloria the keys to our future. With our new rooms, we were fast developing a broader clientele for the restaurant. This meant growing profits to fund ministry and more opportunities to share with customers about who we were and what we believed.

The Lord had again shown His steadfast faithfulness in bringing us through a very dark time in 1998. By late summer of 1999, our fortunes were very much on the upswing.

Rising from the ashes

1999

The media had become a free source of advertising and promotion for our business. Television stations, both local and national, repeatedly came to us to run feature programs. This kind of publicity would have been prohibitively expensive for our small business if we had been paying for the privilege, but the Lord had opened a door to send forth His Word out at no cost.

We were also making strides at the management level. Maria Moraru, whom Jeff had hired, was a hard worker with a good head on her shoulders. She recruited and brought on our first chambermaid. Maria was insistent that we maintain our bed and breakfast rooms immaculately. This became a feature greatly appreciated by our guests, who came from all over Romania, Western Europe, the USA, and Canada. Profits earned from our little B & B allowed us to be of greater help in funding the ministries to which we felt drawn. It did not take a rocket scientist to figure out that our future lay, in large measure, with expanding our little bed and breakfast inn.

Gloria and I sometimes became acquainted with people who were customers at Little Texas, such as the Treptows. The American husband, Kurt, was in his late thirties and ran the Center for Romanian Studies in Iasi. He was a doctoral historian and of some renown for his epic volume *A History of Romania*. Even the Romanians considered this to be the definitive written history of their country. Kurt's wife, Lara, appeared to be in her late twenties and was Romanian. He was partial to our marinated filet mignon; she to our apple pie.

Kurt met with me one day in May 2000 to discuss a proposal from His Excellency James Rosapeppe, US Ambassador to Romania. As well as being connected in high places, Kurt was the embassy's warden for our region. He wanted to know if we would be interested in putting on a July 4th celebration in collaboration with the ambassador. I had already arranged to have a Christian Bluegrass group come to Iasi for ten days during that time. The embassy's proposal seemed like a perfect fit for us, so I readily agreed.

On our next trip to Bucharest to buy things for the restaurant, Gloria and I met with Ambassador Rosapeppe in his office. In a relaxed and casual manner, we discussed the series of upcoming events we were planning for the 4th. He indicated his desire to arrive by private plane to celebrate in Iasi with us. The US ambassador's presence would guarantee that tickets for our event would be in great demand. He gave us his personal assurance that the full weight of the embassy would be behind us in organizing the event. This proved indeed to be the case when we received a letter confirming that a Marine Color Guard would attend as I had requested. This had taken a mere telephone call from the ambassador to the Marine commander.

After weeks of planning and organizing, the day arrived. More than 200 ticket holders attended our soirée. Present also were television, radio, and newspaper crews, all straining to get an interview with the many luminaries seated on every square inch of our garden. The Bluegrass music, courtesy of the Christian band Blue Grace, was a huge hit. The ambassador's wife, Sheila, even accompanied the band on vocals for a rendition of "Amy." The Marine Color Guard performed their ceremony for the "Star-Spangled Banner." Our garden echoed with the crisp, staccato sounds of Marine infantry rifles as the color guard executed their stirring tribute to the red, white, and blue. It was electrifying. At my signal, fireworks then lit up the sky and brought down the house. The next morning's headline read, "The only thing missing at Little Texas was J. R. Ewing." The Lord had given us a tremendous success. We were able to raise thousands of dollars. This helped send many of Iasi's poorest children to a Christian summer camp.

The Lord was to use the week of Blue Grace's visit to set a high standard for what people could do in the community if only the will existed. After the July 4th celebration, we filled the balance of the week with concerts at various venues. Blue Grace played and then shared the gospel with university students, kids at camp, and more than 2,000 prison inmates in

Iasi. A local television station aired a one-hour program of their music, along with candid interviews about the faith that had brought these musicians to Iasi. Clearly, the Lord was doing a new thing in Romania.

In early August 2000, I felt the Lord was leading us to expand our hotel capacity. I began to focus in earnest on what would become a new eight-room wing on the back of our property. I then casually mentioned my plans to Nelu. The next day, he was out on the back property measuring distances and pounding in stakes to get an idea of where best to situate the new building. In addition, he had contacted a geodetic engineer to determine if the soil would support such a large structure. Thrilled with a new construction project, Nelu was like a kid with a new toy. We sketched out the dimensions to allow for a conference room on the floor below, where the terrain sloped abruptly downward from the garden.

I spent the balance of that month estimating what it would cost from ground-breaking to opening. The "guestimate" ended up at $165,000. Not to worry—we already had all of $15,000 in cash to begin this new undertaking. The challenge was how to arrange for the other $145,000 that we would surely need. Thus began another intensive time of seeking the Lord's direction and provision in prayer. I made initial plans for a fundraising trip to the USA in late September. It was essential to push hard once we had broken ground.

On September 1, after receiving our president, Sam Metcalf's and the CRM board's formal approval, we broke ground. A huge backhoe cut a swathe across our wonderfully manicured lawn to reach the area staked out with string where the building would eventually stand. We had begun.

Later that day, Bob telephoned to ask me if he and Radu and Ben Onu, two of his most ardent young disciples, could come and talk to me at the house. Soon we were sitting in our living room and Bob, clearly having been delegated the task, launched into their intended inquiry. The Onu boys had a vision to start a business to support the ever-growing and deepening ministry of Ecclesia. They would help finance Radu in his role as a full-time Christian evangelist-cum-pastor. It sounded like a fine plan to me.

Bob then explained that they specifically wanted to buy a piece of land

and build some houses for resale. The land was in an ideal area of Iasi. The project's investors and the ministry would share the profits. The sticking point was that they had a piece of property in mind but needed $15,000 to secure it. They needed the money that day. Bob then delivered the punch line. Could I/Little Texas put up the $15,000?

I sat there quietly for some moments before I began to pray silently. I immediately sensed that the Lord was in this project, but the devil was in the details. How could I give the only funds we had for the hotel to an entirely different project? Was this prudent? Were they kidding?

Following that prolonged pause, I simply sighed and said, "Sure, we can do that." After all, helping to launch new businesses as missions was a fundamental part of our strategy. Ben and Radu were the kind of key nationals whose vision we sought to empower. This would, however, mean starting the Little Texas expansion with no funds.

Fortunately, during my time later that month in the USA, the expansion idea immediately drew support from churches and others. This dynamic seemed to reinforce the concept that nothing attracts further consideration like a prior "success." We were, in fact, expanding on our base operation in building-block fashion. While by no means an effortless undertaking, the entire process never had the feeling of being overwhelming, for which I was extremely grateful. We even benefit from a Romanian investment tax-credit loophole that would mean a $40,000 savings to the building project.

Part of our vision for Little Texas was to seek out relationships for evangelistic purposes. Having worked so hard and been through so much together for the Independence Day celebration that year, we began to get to know Dr. Kurt Treptow, the doctoral historian, and his wife, Lara, better. At first, we had them to dinner at Little Texas, and then to our home for an evening together. Kurt had apparently put my name down to become a member of the Romanian Rotary Club in Iasi. Ready or not, I joined the Rotary Club. This now afforded me time each week with Kurt, to say nothing of the other Rotarians, all Romanian business leaders. I found this fundamentally fulfilling since it had been a prayer of mine from the inception of Little Texas. We wanted to influence that unreached people group, "the haves." Almost every other ministry seemed focused on the other 85 per cent of Iasi, "the have-nots," and rightly so. Consequently, our calling and position in the community was somewhat of an anomaly.

In April 2001, our home church in Orange, California sent a short-term mission group of thirteen to take part in our ministry. The group included our senior pastor, Bob Burris, and Gerimic Meier, a young general contractor. Some of the others were new to the church since we had left for Romania in January 1993. It was a kind of reunion for us, as a few in the group were long-time friends like Lee and Mary Beth Ramlo. Lee was a craftsman and ended up designing the entrance to the new wing.

Our home church had also brought needed funds for the hotel expansion. Several among the group toiled for days alongside our Romanian workers on the interior. Principally, they mounted the ceiling wood that became our trademark.

The advent of spring 2001 also meant having to find a way to say goodbye to Bob and Vicki McCuistion. Their decade-long tenure in Romania was coming to a close. Quite literally, this was the end of an era. The McCuistions were beloved by all who knew them. For ten years, they had selflessly poured out their lives into the next generation of Romanian Christian leaders. These disciples would now carry the torch into tomorrow. Bob and Vicki shared a rich legacy of lives impacted, inspired, transformed, and mobilized for greater acts of Kingdom service. In May, we planned a huge farewell party at Little Texas to honor their family. The bash was our gift to this extraordinary couple who had become, in many ways, closer than family.

Our son Trevor had returned to Iasi with us in early 1999. In June 2001, he too completed his high-school home studies. In that month, we flew with him to the USA for the first step in preparing him for college and his new life away from home.

Shortly before we left the USA to head back to Iasi, Maria Moraru contacted me by email. The new eight-room wing was finished and we had already received reservation requests. She wanted to know if they could let out the new rooms ahead of schedule and before our return. I could not type an affirmative response fast enough. So it was that, fifty-one weeks after breaking ground on our biggest project to date, we received our first, very grateful, hotel guests in the new wing.

Teach your children well

In early September 2001, I made an appointment with Liliana Romaniuc, the director of the Richard Wurmbrand Christian School. We had supported the school since its inception in 1995 and I tried to keep up with its progress. Liliana was a remarkable woman of great vision. As a woman leader in a male-dominated world, she had paid a price for her Christian stand in developing the vision of the school. Seated in her tastefully appointed office, Liliana proceeded to share with me the most recent installment of just how great that cost had become.

For some time, Liliana had been counseling Alina, a top student now entering her senior year. Liliana had sensed that there was a problem at home, but had been unable to divine its true nature. Then one day, a very distraught Alina broke down in tears in Liliana's office. After gentle urging, the tawdry tale unfolded. Alina's mother had divorced and then remarried some years earlier. It now became apparent that Alina's stepfather had been sexually abusing her for years. During her time at the Christian school, Alina had come to Christ and was growing in her faith. With that moral compass now to guide her, she knew that what was happening at home was an aberration.

Liliana was convinced that Alina's story was true. As the headmistress and guardian of the school's vision, she was faced with a thorny dilemma. After much prayer, she contacted the proper public authorities and laid out the situation. Given the school's stellar reputation, the case received a fair hearing. Things turned ugly, however, when the stepfather learned of the accusations. The scandal soon broke in the local newspapers. Accusations of "brainwashing" were, not for the first time, bandied about in the press. An Orthodox priest was most vehemently vocal about the Christian "proselytizers." Those in positions of civic academic leadership were reluctant to back the school. Lawsuits were prepared. School board members received threatening telephone calls. Sinister forces were at work behind the scenes.

A series of meetings took place. These culminated in a showdown between both sides in Liliana's office. Present were Alina, her parents, two

Orthodox priests, Department of Education heads, Liliana, and television cameras. It all came down to Alina being asked to take back her story and recant her new faith. In the crucible of fire, before the cameras, Alina stood by her faith and her story. She bravely recounted all the sordid details of what had become the norm in her life. It was now apparent that the mother had known all along, but had simply refused to act for fear of "losing her man." Alina reiterated her faith in Christ. When she finished, the room was deathly quiet. Those present began to distance themselves from the stepfather. A formal ruling would be forthcoming. Upon leaving, one of the priests remarked to Liliana, "This is the kind of school where I would like to send my daughter."

The court ruled in the school's favor. The school helped Alina move into a small apartment with another high-school student and a woman on staff. Alina would go on to graduate with honors. Later, she would move to Italy and start a new life. This was how they were saved, one life at a time.

By late October 2001, we were hitting our stride at Little Texas and reaping the spoils of the Lord's bounty. The opening of the new eight rooms had more than doubled our monthly net profits to help fund ministry. This was a blessed and welcome development. I sensed, however, that we were far from through. Following Bob and Vicki's move back to the USA, CRM had purchased their old home. They had hoped to use it in some way for ministry. It had sat empty since the late spring. With our house situated right next door to Little Texas, we became convinced that we needed to move out and convert our home into more hotel rooms.

We worked with an architect to transform our old home on paper into three suites and a private dining room. Later, in a short telephone conversation with Sam Metcalf, we were given the go-ahead. Nelu began the vigorous renovation of our two-story house. Hardly had I spoken the words that we were to move ahead, when he launched into the demolishing of walls as the first step in the process. Reinvested Little Texas revenue and tax savings almost entirely funded the $36,000 project cost. Additionally, FiloCalia invested $5,000 towards the project. Their investment would provide them with an additional income stream, as they were to share in the future profits from the three suites.

Sometime earlier, Gloria and I had gifted our one-half interest in the first store space (FiloMarket) to FiloCalia, as well as our ownership of the Gloria store. They had sold the first store, so I was anxious to suggest the investment idea to them before those funds could be otherwise spent. On behalf of the FiloCalia board, Bogdan immediately accepted my offer. We put the funds to work finishing the three additional suites. On a roll with the new expansion, I felt as if we were continuing to position ourselves well for the long-term.

In November 2001, missionary Dan Onu, brother of Radu and Ben, invited me to accompany him to Moldova. He had moved into Moldova to help with a new church plant in the town of Taul. Argentin, another of our key missionaries, had originally come from that town to attend university in Iasi. Due to the influence and discipleship of Ecclesia, Argentin had returned to Taul as a full-time missionary. We had also recruited, trained, and sent out Florin, once a waiter at Little Texas, with his wife, Kati, to Taul. The couple lived in a small mission house that we had purchased for the ministry. Our Christian businesses in Iasi were helping to support all of the work there.

The ministry was now bearing fruit. The new church plant in Taul had planned a special service for the installation of elders, and Dan asked me to join him for the occasion. We rented a Moldovan taxi, deeming it safer, given the bandits who roamed the back roads of the untamed country.

Although only November, it was already freezing cold. From the home of Florin and Kati, we shuffled through the darkness and glue-like mud to the little house where the church met. Some thirty people gathered for the worship time. Most were new believers. In Moldova, there was no such thing as "transfer growth;" this was the only Christian church for miles around. Once gathered, we fellowshipped as one in a stark room over which dangled a single bare light bulb. Truly, it was "the steak, not the sizzle," that brought these faithful out to church. Icy wind seeped through the mud-and-straw brick wall. The only heat emanated from a too-small wood-burning stove in a corner. None of this seemed to matter, as I watched the Holy Spirit transform the lack of trappings into a holy assemblage.

After the service, I greeted a man in his early fifties. We began to chat in the easy manner of brothers in Christ. The deep furrows and traces in his face told of a hard life. I listened as he spoke of his new habit of rising at midnight to thank God for the privilege of worshipping Him. His name was Necolia. He had been Taul's town drunk. When nothing else had been at hand, 90 proof rubbing alcohol had been his drink of choice. His life, and that of his family, had been a disaster.

Two years earlier, Necolia had grudgingly accepted our missionary Argentin's invitation to a Christian summer camp near Taul. It was there that Necolia gave his life to Christ. He stopped drinking immediately upon conversion. Skilled with a tractor, Necolia then found his first job in years through a contact at that same camp. This was a remarkable occurrence, as jobs in Moldova were scarce. Necolia became a good husband and father. He grew in the Lord and later became a deacon in the Taul church. As you might imagine, his radical conversion, as evidenced by his sobriety, caused no small stir in that tiny rural hamlet.

My chat with Necolia served to reaffirm and fuel my call to ministry. As the businesses succeeded and grew, we were increasingly able to provide resources to fund the work of bringing the lost and hopeless to faith in Christ.

Opportunity in Nashville

2001–2002

Thanksgiving was now upon us. We had managed to keep up our annual family Thanksgiving tradition during our years in Romania. This year, we would be hosting Gerimie and Sofia Meier, a thirty-something couple from our home church in Orange, California. Gerimie was an ex-Marine-turned-builder, and had been part of the team from the church that had come in April. Together with Sofia, he had managed to grow a successful company, while growing two children on the home front. I first met the Meiers during a visit to our Orange church; I had spoken there about our ministry and the many ways in which the Lord was at work.

After my talk, the Meiers decided to come and visit Iasi. The Lord used the further exposure to His work in Romania and Moldova like a cosmic tractor beam, inexorably drawing Gerimie and Sofia ever closer to His purposes there. Ben and Radu Onu, the brothers who had had the vision to expand their home-building business, expressed a desire to have a builder from the West work with them. The Meiers' example was to be a testament to others of what was required to live in obedience to the Lord.

In keeping with our vision, Gloria and I continued to develop relationships through Little Texas. Kurt and Lara Treptow became our good friends. The four of us routinely spent evenings together. We ate dinner, played cards, or sometimes watched a movie or concert on Kurt's state-of-the-art sound system. We really enjoyed this growing friendship.

Lara had traveled several times with Kurt to the USA on his frequent trips. As she shared her impressions from their travels, it was apparent that she liked America a great deal. One night over dinner, Kurt mentioned his next trip, planned for early February 2002. Lara indicated that she would not be accompanying him. Kurt pressed her a bit about her reasons for staying behind. She admitted being tired and that she had no desire to go through the jet lag again any time soon. They dropped the matter, although we sensed that Kurt was disappointed.

We too were due to leave for the USA at that time, to attend a missions conference at First Evangelical Church in Memphis. Quite by coincidence, we ended up on the same flight with Kurt from Bucharest to Amsterdam. I sat across the aisle from him and we chatted for the entire flight. He expressed his disappointment that Lara had not made the trip. Soon we parted, but we promised to get together as soon as we were all back in Iasi.

First Evangelical Church of Memphis had invited us, along with Valentin Chirica, the head of the Way of Joy ministry, to attend their missions conference. We especially looked forward to this conference, as Pastor Ronnie Stevens had accepted the senior pastor position at First Evangelical some years earlier. His presence in Memphis meant we had an ardent proponent of our ministry (and of us as missionaries) at one of our key churches.

Ronnie took it upon himself to arrange a meeting for us with the parents of his new son-in-law. Chick and Andi Hill agreed to have lunch with us near the offices of Mr. Hill's hotel company, The Davidson Group. Chick's firm owned or ran more than two dozen major hotel properties nationwide. Gloria and I had mentioned to Ronnie that we really felt that some training at a high-end hotel could greatly enhance our systems and improve services at Little Texas. So he asked us to tell our story, in brief, to this gracious couple.

When I spoke about doing business locally to support ministry in Iasi, Mrs. Hill leaned forward and, in her quiet voice, exclaimed, "I have never heard of such an idea from a missionary!" The concept seemed to intrigue her. When I finished, Ronnie then prodded, "So tell them what you need, Jeri." Usually this is where a missionary requests a substantial sum of money. In this case, however, I went on to explain to the Hills that what we actually needed was a hotel complex where we could further train and learn about the business. In response, Mr. Hill thought for a moment and then suggested that their Nashville Sheraton would probably be a good property for such purposes. He then offered to put us up and make his staff available for any of our needs. Finally he asked, "Is that all you need?"

I was so taken aback by such an amazing offer that it took me a moment to formulate a response. I finally said, "Do you know how much this will do for our business?" It was more of a statement than a question. The Lord was continuing to provide just the right opportunity at just the right time.

Almost immediately upon returning to Iasi, we learned from Kurt that Lara had left him. He insisted that he had no idea why she had done so. Over the following month, I visited him often at his apartment in the evenings. Usually Petronela and Dana, two of his employees, were also there. Petronela confided to me that Kurt had been threatening to take his life. From the first night at his apartment, Kurt shared that he felt there was no hope in life and absolutely no future. I used the crisis to open up to him about the hope and future found in Jesus Christ. He seemed attentive and interested in what I was saying. Many nights I would not leave his place until well after midnight.

Then the news came. Lara had contacted Kurt through her attorney. She was filing for divorce. Gloria and I were as equally concerned about Lara as we were about Kurt. We wanted to reach out to her in some way. Through Kurt's attorney, we obtained an address for her, and drove to see her unannounced. As we visited, Lara shared the painful truth about her marriage to Kurt. She revealed his addiction to pornography and how it had cast a shadow over their eight years together. Her attempts to confront him were consistently rebuffed with claims that there was nothing wrong with such a pastime. To Lara's credit, she seemed hesitant to speak poorly of Kurt. We reassured her that we were her friends as well as Kurt's and that we wanted to help if we could.

That night, I again met with Kurt at his apartment across town. Sharing about our meeting with Lara, I told him of her assertion that he knew exactly why she had left. He then admitted his problem with pornography. He said he needed help, so I also reassured him of my willingness to do what I could. A sense of dread filled Gloria and me. Each day, an ever-thickening plot was becoming more convoluted.

Gloria and I were now due in Nashville. Mr. Chick Hill, the hotel magnate we had met through Ronnie Stevens, had arranged a ten-day training stint for us at his downtown Sheraton. During our stay, we were all over the twenty-five-story complex. The Sheraton staff were professional, helpful, and extremely accommodating. We took copious notes and created a thick file of their procedures and systems.

While observing the kitchen crew, we became acquainted with Michael LaBar, an amiable man in his thirties. While he worked, he shared recipes and tips from the culinary world that would be of great help to us. Chef Michael brightened when he learned that we were missionaries. He and his wife, Vashti, attended a nearby Baptist church. Michael had been asking the Lord to show him ways he might use his skills as a chef for the Kingdom. My mind began to race with possibilities. We arranged to meet him and his wife at their home one afternoon. Astonishingly, both seemed open to the idea of visiting Romania to help us at Little Texas.

When our time came to an end, we said our goodbyes to the great folks at the Sheraton. We promised Michael that we would keep in touch and pray about a visit for him to Iasi some day.

The case against Kurt Treptow

September 2002

Just because I'm paranoid, doesn't mean they're not after me. (Anon.)

Back we went to Romania, eager to share all we had learned at the Nashville Sheraton. This training greatly helped our staff progress at Little Texas. At the same time, on all ministry fronts, the Lord was blessing the work of our hands. In Moldova, people were coming to Christ and new leaders were emerging. That still-Communist stronghold was fertile ground for the gospel. A former Soviet satellite, it had been Russia's factory for massive orders of giant machine parts. Their economy had depended totally on the Russian colossus. With the Soviet collapse, Moldova's economy virtually imploded. From a population of five million, more than one million had fled the country in the years following 1989. In the aftermath of such a market vacuum, economic and social upheaval, the Mafia had become entrenched. They would prove to be increasingly virulent and violent, an ever-present cancer in the very marrow of that shaken society.

Part of Ecclesia's vision was to send Romanian missionaries to such foreign fields. As part of this vision, it had sent out Dan Onu, Argentin, and Florin and Kati. In the capital, Chisiniev, Dan did the work of training young disciples, who lived with him in his apartment. He traveled weekly several hours by bus to Taul, serving the growing new church fellowship. Their vision was to plant other churches in towns like Taul where no Christian church existed. We, of course, wanted to be a part of this new vision. Little Texas had given the money for Dan to buy a used vehicle. I made plans to again visit Moldova in November 2002. Since my first foray into that turbulent neighboring country, I had a sense that the Lord was preparing for a great harvest there. Dan foresaw that it was time to recruit workers and pray for the resources to bring in that rich harvest. Anointed nationals of such profound vision had always been a draw to me. We would focus much of our future efforts on empowering the work in Moldova.

On September 17, 2002, I was gliding through a thoroughly unremarkable day. I had tinkered at this and that, making it home in time to have lunch with Gloria. Then Kurt Treptow telephoned. He was en route to Iasi from Bucharest and wanted to meet me. He would call me that evening when he arrived in town.

Late that night, my telephone awakened me from a sound sleep. The voice simply told me to call a certain telephone number. Groggy and puzzled, I dutifully punched the number given to me into my telephone. I identified myself to the voice on the other end. It turned out to be Liviu Bran, Kurt's attorney. Kurt had given him my name. Now I was wide awake. Liviu went on to say that the authorities were in the process of arresting Kurt. He asked me to meet him in his office at 7 a.m. the next day. I pressed Liviu for details, but he insisted that he could not talk on the telephone. Whatever the explanation, I would have to wait for another few hours.

Making my way downtown the next morning, I knocked on Liviu's door and was let in by his secretary. Also present were Dana and Petronela, Kurt's employees. Their tense smiles could not mask the shock in their eyes. While I sipped strong coffee, Liviu leaned forward with his hands folded. As if reciting scripted testimony, he began to relate the events of the past twelve hours. Liviu informed me that Kurt was the subject of a very serious criminal investigation. The entire vice squad had raided Kurt's Center for Romanian Studies, spending hours doing a search-and-seizure operation under a written warrant.

Liviu's brow furrowed and his eyes narrowed before he gave me the bottom line. "The police have in their possession pornographic videotapes, some with young children involved. Mr. Jeri, only if God gives a miracle does Kurt have a chance of avoiding prison." He then paused to hear my response. "Do you mean to say that Kurt produced these videos?" I asked incredulously. Liviu, ever the legal eagle, avoided the question. Instead, he launched into his defense strategy. The first step was to telephone a highly placed government official. This turned out to be Kurt's good friend, the Romanian Secretary of Defense. Liviu managed to reach the Minister's wife. He proceeded to explain the current dilemma and received a promise that the message would be passed on to the Defense Minister. Liviu then promised to contact me later in the day when he had further information.

I tried to concentrate on the day's work, but my mind kept brooding over what a major scandal this could be if it broke to the press. At 3:30, my cell phone rang as I was driving across town. It was Liviu with a message from Kurt. He said that everything was fine and wondered if I could meet Kurt that night at his apartment. I pressed for details, but Liviu cut me short, insisting that Kurt would explain everything that evening.

All of this still bewildered me as I entered the rickety elevator later in the day and made my way to the seventh floor. Dana let me in. Kurt came into the entryway, wearing flannel pajamas, a baseball cap, and a contrite smile. As we shook hands, he shook his head saying, "Well, I'm just glad that this is all over." Once in his private sitting room, I asked him how it could have been resolved, given the overwhelming body of evidence in police custody. Literally, the entire vice squad had taken part in the raid on Kurt's headquarters. Kurt leaned forward and spoke in a quiet tone. He explained that his friend, the Secretary of Defense, had made a call to the Prime Minister. The Prime Minister then telephoned the chief of police in Iasi and instructed him to release Kurt and drop the case. "So it's over," he said with a deep sigh. "Let me tell you, Jeri, it was a horrible experience being all night in a prison cell." I believed him.

Driving home that night, 2 Peter 2:19 came to my mind: "for a man is a slave to whatever has mastered him." In getting off like this, Kurt would not be forced to confront his private demons. The authorities had freed him from prison, but he remained a prisoner to his own obsessions. This was not "over" by a long shot.

The following Wednesday, Kurt called me again. His voice sounded agitated and strained. "I need to see you when I get to Iasi. It's urgent! I must speak to you in private." I told him to call me when he reached Iasi. I stayed up late, waiting for a telephone call that never came. Early the next morning, September 20, I received a telephone call from Nelu. He asked me if I had seen the news on television. I had not, so he instructed me to buy a paper at a newsstand. Grabbing a paper at one of the many kiosks, I gaped at the front page, which showed a full color picture of Kurt's face. In boldface type the headline read: "American Agent Arrested in Iasi!"

The same day, the news trumpeted the mysterious disappearance of Kurt Treptow. The media put a rather sinister spin on their first report of what they called the "Treptow Case." Conspiracy theories abounded. One alleged that Kurt was an agent for the CIA. The Romanian parliament was hotly debating the case. One anonymous MP was quoted as saying, "Agent Kurt Treptow was the instrument, corrupt and blackmailable, of the Secret Service and by who knows who else ..."

The search for Kurt intensified as alleged victims, both boys and girls, began to come forward. It was at this time that the media focused on Tatiana, a woman working in Kurt's office. Allegedly, she had approached these minors, offering them money to appear in pornographic videos clandestinely filmed at Kurt's Center. Adrian Tuca, the "Larry King" of Romania (complete with suspenders and silver microphone), dedicated an entire program on national television to the "Treptow Case." The case had now achieved the status of a bona fide nationwide scandal. The press continued to crank out scathing full-page accounts of the heinous deeds, along with full-length photos of Tatiana in the nude. In typical Romanian tabloid fashion, only her eyes were covered.

About this time, I began to receive telephone calls from reporters seeking my comments. It was no secret that Kurt and I were friends. With the disappearance of Kurt, the media was circling me like sharks. The *Monitorul* ran a picture of Kurt on the terrace of Little Texas taken the previous May. The article spoke of "Little Texas being owned by another well-known American, Jeri Little." Things were now hitting close to home. I was beginning to wonder if our association would somehow directly implicate me.

On October 2, Adrian Nastase, the Prime Minister, stood before cameras and took spirited questions on the case. President Iliescu denounced Kurt for his alleged crimes. The Minister of Defense, Mr. Talpes, heretofore a close friend of Kurt's, declined comment. From the top down, it was now clear that Kurt Treptow was persona non grata. Everyone was running for political cover, and Kurt was still missing.

Two weeks had now passed since Kurt first disappeared. Rumors were flying regarding "Kurt sightings." The media called me constantly. At last, I turned my cell phone off. One day on the street, I was accosted by an insistent and out-of-breath reporter. Shoving a microphone in my face, she asked for my comment about Kurt. "I have been trying to find you for three days," she practically gasped. "What can you tell me about Kurt Treptow?" In a measured tone, I told her that Kurt had a God-sized hole in his life that only a personal relationship with Jesus Christ could fill. I told her that I was praying for Kurt and hoped that he would find the peace that Jesus offered. In response, the reporter clicked off the recorder, thanked me without conviction, and walked away. The next day there was no sign of my quote in her story.

I tried to continue my work at Little Texas the best I could. Each day, I had a daily briefing with Maria, our general manager. One particular morning, we sat in the conference room and went through the week's reservations and group bookings. Consulting her list, Maria hesitated before bringing up the last item. With a pained expression, she began to tell me what was on her mind. I could see that she was extremely agitated.

At length, Maria explained that two agents who had recently been frequenting Little Texas had approached Dan Sbangu, one of our top waiters. One was with the Romanian CIA and the other with the American FBI. They had arranged to meet Dan for coffee in another part of town. Maria inhaled deeply before proceeding. "They swore Dan to secrecy, saying it could go badly for him if he divulged details of their talk." They asked Dan to keep an eye out for suspicious activity at Little Texas. Such an establishment was seen as a good front for trafficking in pornographic materials. I found all of this preposterous, but said nothing.

Maria concluded with, "Jeri, you are under surveillance. Your phones are no doubt tapped, you are being followed, and your email is probably being intercepted." I could see by the anguish etched on her face that she was almost at the end of her rope. At that moment, I had the strange sensation of dangling by one myself. Feigning calm, I tried to reassure Maria that all would be well. After all, I had nothing to hide. Over the years, Maria had become quite well known in Iasi for her position as general manager at Little Texas. She was concerned about what all this might mean for her personally. With a tad more conviction than I felt, I told her that she had nothing to worry about. Not yet, anyway.

I left Maria and headed home to share the cheery news with Gloria. Not surprisingly, she took it all in with typical equanimity. We prayed together for the Lord's protection and wisdom. Later that day, we ran errands in the city. Upon returning, as we drove up our tiny alley, there were two men down at the corner watching the house. I got out of my ancient Mercedes, opened the gate, and pulled in the driveway. We grabbed our packages and made our way into the house. The next day's newspaper report told of "a mysterious couple who sped up to a secluded home in Ticou; a man in dark sunglasses alighted from his Mercedes and raced into the house before we could ply him with questions." This was the product of someone's overactive imagination. Nonetheless, we began to feel trapped.

On Wednesday evening of the same week, Gloria attended a Sunday school teachers' meeting. While she was gone, I heard a noise in the front yard. I grabbed my walking stick to go investigate. Four shadowy figures stood in the dark on my front walkway. Dressed in my slippers and bathrobe, I demanded to know who they were. A voice from their midst identified them as reporters from the *Monitorul*. I asked them why they were in my yard and what they wanted. Timidly, the one closest said that they wanted to know where Kurt Treptow was. They suspected that I was hiding him in our house. I responded that I had no idea where Kurt was. I went on to tell them that they had no business invading my privacy. At this, they moved back towards the gate. Mumbling some semblance of an apology, the foursome melted back into the same shadows from which they had emerged.

The front page of the *Monitorul* the next morning splashed a full-color photo of our house with the caption "The lair where Kurt Treptow is hiding." At Little Texas, everyone was abuzz with the news. I spoke to Maria and my management team to reassure them that the article was pure fiction. There was nothing in the manual on cross-cultural missions to cover such a situation. I took a drive to do a mental assessment of my predicament. In a nutshell, the media were hounding us, they suspected that my house was the hideout for the fugitive Kurt Treptow, and people suspected me of complicity in an international pornography ring. In addition, the US FBI and Romanian CIA were investigating me and asking one of my employees to spy on me, they tapped my telephones, and intercepted my emails. And no, this was not a bad dream.

At the time, a mission team from Alabama was in Iasi doing dental ministry. Fred Judd, the team leader, had a great heart for missions. He had my complete confidence. He also had an international cell phone. For all three reasons, I asked Fred to come to my house that afternoon. I hoped to call Sam Metcalf without "Big Brother" listening in. A groggy Sam answered the telephone after several minutes—it was still only 4 a.m. in California. I quickly went through the entire scenario. Sam had no suggestions to offer, but it was still encouraging to hear his sleepy voice. Trying to lighten the situation, I asked him to check the CRM manual to see if my employee benefits remained in force during foreign incarceration. It was good to share a laugh. More serious moments were sure to follow.

The acid test

October 2002

... I was in prison and you came to visit me. (Matthew 25:36)

Kurt was initially incarcerated in Bucharest. A month later, he was transferred to Iasi. Kurt would stand trial in the county where the alleged crimes had taken place. His attorney, Liviu, confided to me that the chief prosecutor and Kurt's enemies "were closing in for the kill." Still under investigation myself, I did not want to know anything more that might be later used against me. Now in the prison in Iasi, Kurt was only minutes away. He was closer, but would the authorities grant me or anyone else access? In the press, the rumor mill was running full tilt. They gave much ink to speculation regarding the mysterious Tatiana and the trial's outcome.

I was soon to learn that our American embassy would play a part in Kurt's case, as a matter of due process. As part of the embassy's American Citizen Services Department function, this was protocol when Americans ran afoul of the law in foreign countries. (If I had known of such embassy services earlier, I might have had an easier time during my car accident situation in 1994.)

Ironically, in Kurt's stead, the embassy had asked Gloria and I to serve as the American embassy warden for our region. This required a meeting with Jay Smith, the current Consul General. He introduced us to the Third Secretary, Bill Sullivan, who handled the American Citizen Services department for Romania. Bill was informal and friendly as he explained his role and specific duties. After this, he leaned forward and nonchalantly began to outline his latest task. This consisted of visiting Iasi periodically to monitor Kurt Treptow's case and his treatment. Bill mentioned that he would be visiting Iasi soon and on a regular basis. Ever the capitalist, I suggested he stay at Little Texas and take advantage of our discount for diplomats.

I met with Bill Sullivan over breakfast at Little Texas when he made his first visit. He confirmed our fear that some inmates had beaten Kurt up. Suspected child molesters fared poorly in prison. The thought of what Kurt must be going through shook me. I began to share my faith with Bill. He professed to be a believing Lutheran and readily sympathized with my desire to reach Kurt for Christ. He suggested that I speak to the warden about visiting Kurt, since I knew him from the summer prison concerts with Blue Grace two years earlier.

During this time, Nelu was working speedily with our crew on the Way of Joy space renovation. The original space was being expanded and refurbished.

The time had come to inaugurate the new Way of Joy facilities. The mercury plummeted and the first snow fell the very day that renovations were complete. More than fifty expectant children and adults were present for the ribbon-cutting ceremony (a tradition in Romania), which took place in the tiny courtyard. After a quick snip, everyone filed inside to inspect the handiwork. Following prayers of dedication, we served refreshments out of the new kitchen. It was fulfilling to have embarked on this project just two months earlier and now be able to see it come to fruition shortly before we would be going home to the USA for Christmas. Our friend and President of the County Board, Mr. Flaiser, spoke to the crowd on behalf of the city leaders. In a simple, yet heartfelt, way, he expressed admiration for such an undertaking. It was a great start to a new era for the Way of Joy ministry.

By contacting Mr. Bors, the prison warden, I was able to arrange a meeting with Kurt. Graciously, the warden allowed me to meet Kurt in his spacious office. Two black-clad ninja types, hired as bodyguards, ushered Kurt in. There had been threats on his life. The warden busied himself with paperwork at his desk. Kurt was now clean-shaven and looked as if he had recovered from at least some of the initial ordeal. As we chatted across a coffee table, I asked him if he had been reading the Bible I had given him. He indicated that the Scriptures had kept him "alive and sane." I only stayed twenty minutes or so, not wanting to abuse the privilege. After thanking Mr. Bors and saying goodbye to Kurt, I left, hoping to be able to see him again before our departure in two weeks. I decided to go straight home, anxious to see Gloria and share the news. On the way, I prayed, mentally replaying the video of my time with Kurt. He seemed to be moving towards a genuine relationship with God. I prayed for the days ahead and the outcome of the trial. I prayed too that Kurt would, come what might, give his life to Jesus. Lastly, I prayed for one last chance to see Kurt ahead of the verdict in the trial, due that first week of December.

The verdict

December 2002

It was now early December. With less than a week before we were to leave Iasi for the USA, I decided to contact prison warder Mr. Bors. In the past, Little Texas had sponsored different projects for the teenage inmates. To that end, I wanted to offer again some holiday cheer for the more than sixty detainees between the ages of fourteen and eighteen. In the prison population, there were minor offenders and hardened felons.

Mr. Bors seemed delighted with my well-timed offer. As it so happened, December 6 was the day when the prison would put on their Christmas program. Unfortunately, they had not been successful in attracting a sponsor for the celebration. So Little Texas put up a sum of money to ensure that each youth would receive a package of goodies, which I would distribute at the end of the pageant. I agreed to attend that morning and take part in the festivities.

After discussing the celebration, I asked Mr. Bors if it might be possible for me to visit Kurt one last time before I left the country. His response was non-committal. There had been significant pressure from high places for Mr. Bors to show no favoritism towards his now infamous American detainee.

On the day of the program, the guards seated me in the prison youth club and asked me to make some remarks to the hundred or so participants. After this, they led me to the front to hand out the Christmas packages. I smiled at each youthful face in turn, thinking all the while that any one of them could have been Marcus or Trevor. When I finished, I felt a tug at my elbow. On Mr. Bors's whispered command, a uniformed guard escorted me to a tiny adjacent craft room. The guard told me I had only a few minutes. I sensed someone approaching from behind. It was Kurt. He was dressed in military fatigues and wore a wool hat against the cold. He seemed so relaxed and at ease, exuding confidence that he would be acquitted.

I took that cue to remind him that, even if the authorities released him, his problem would not go away. He would need a great deal of counseling to be healed. I asked if he was still reading the Bible. He said that he had read the entire New Testament and was well into the Old Testament. I then inquired whether, through all of his searching, there had been a point when he had confessed his sins and accepted Christ as his Savior. Without hesitation, Kurt professed, "I have received forgiveness and have Jesus as my Savior. I am a Christian." Knowing our time was short, I prayed for Kurt and promised to keep in touch from the USA. The door to the cramped room then opened and the guard led me back outside.

The next day, as Gloria packed for our three-month trip, the telephone rang. It was Kurt's employee Petronela. She was nervous, waiting for the trial verdict to come in. Third Secretary Bill Sullivan was again staying with us; he also had been awaiting the trial's outcome. At three in the afternoon, I went over to Little Texas. Hunched together in a booth were attorney Liviu, Bill, Dana, and Petronela. Each one had a very long face. Liviu then informed me that the jury had come back with a guilty verdict. Worse still, the judge had "thrown the book" at Kurt. He had received a seven-year prison sentence. I asked how this was possible.

Liviu, pale and resigned, leaned back and let out a long breath before answering, "Jeri, the accused would only receive that sentence if he had either shown absolutely no remorse for his crimes or had literally cursed the judge." He added, "And neither was the case in this instance. This was a message sent and received. This was a lynching, pure and simple."

In the wake of the verdict, the press had a field day. They portrayed Kurt on the front page of the paper as a caricature court jester complete with rattle. The headline read, "Sapte Anii Dupa Gratii": "Seven Years Behind Bars." All of Iasi was abuzz with the news. The court had awarded damages of $50,000 to the families of the victims. Payment of said damages would be, not surprisingly, problematic. Petronela was certain that Kurt would not survive seven years in prison. She was convinced that he would end up taking his own life.

I asked Liviu how this would reflect on his own career. He had a wife and a small child to think about. Liviu said, "Jeri, I am the attorney that got the book thrown at his client, the maximum sentence possible ... Who now is going to want to retain such counsel?" Although I did sympathize with

Liviu, this was, however, an occupational hazard, all the more hazardous in the case of a national sex scandal.

The authorities would allow Kurt four visits per month. Knowing that Petronela and Dana would do the honors, I wrote Kurt a short letter, fumbling to write something that could not be given expression. I have no recollection of the contents of that message. I only hoped that the thought would count for a man who was clearly down for the count. Kurt now had only his new faith to sustain him. I prayed that the Lord would be his sufficiency in the dark and difficult days ahead.

Bethel real-estate venture

2003

Although stunned by the verdict, we needed to focus on our task in the USA. On another visit to Memphis, we reconnected with Sheraton executive chef Michael LaBar. We arranged for his and Vashti's visit to Little Texas the next summer. Our prayer was that the Lord might provide us with an ongoing culinary expert like Michael. Time would tell.

In the spring of 2003, Ben and Radu approached me about expanding their real-estate endeavors. The Meiers had by now moved to Romania and Gerimie was helping to introduce newer building techniques. The time seemed propitious, but I wanted to make sure that we had clear understanding of what profits would go to ministry. How the deals were structured would be essential in avoiding complications. We also needed to keep in mind that it would be necessary to raise capital for further ventures. Over a period of several weeks we met, discussed, haggled, and debated all aspects. In the end, we came up with a workable model. It was not, however, one that I felt would be reproducable. We decided to attract investors who would put up the funds and share in the hoped-for profits. It would provide for 25 per cent of gross profits to be given directly to the ministry of Ecclesia, overseen by myself, Radu, Ben and Gerimie serving as a stewardship team. The remaining 75 per cent of the profit would be returned to investors after their initial capital. In this way, our initial ventures yielded a substantial return to investors who took part. Furthermore, each home built provided nearly $10,000 in profits for ministry.

After four such homes had been sold, we met to determine how to give to the ministry. Our priority was supporting national missionaries and church-planting projects. This continued our original vision of "leveraged stewardship": giving or investing and having that gift return manifold back to the ministry. This began with the donation of clothing in 1992. Our original investment of $15,000 to open the first store had generated nearly $1,000,000 in profits for ministry. Such leverage continued with donations to start Little Texas, which was now returning those funds many times over. Now we furthered that initiative through our real-estate ventures. Since, as we saw it, God was doing the building, we decided to call this "Bethel [House of God] Real Estate."

Chef Michael and Vashti's arrival in Iasi heralded a new phase for Little Texas. He worked with our kitchen crew on new techniques and dishes that became Little Texas standards.

Our July 4th celebration that year also took place during Michael and Vashti's visit. We had 190 guests booked for a sit-down dinner on our terrace. It was, of course, a fundraising event. We had a live band and a fireworks show all lined up.

For the program, we had sixteen of Valentin's Way of Joy children up on stage, each wearing a white T-shirt with the Statue of Liberty on the front. They sang "America the Beautiful" to the crowd. The object of our charity was to send a total of ninety-five of these underprivileged kids to a Way of Joy Christian summer camp the following week.

We always invited VIPs to these types of events and, as per Romanian custom, did not require them to pay for their tickets. To me, it was a rather galling reality of the social pecking order in Romania that those with the greatest wealth paid nothing. One person in this category was the mayor, Senator Solcano. At one point in the evening, he called me over to his table. I was expecting to field some sort of complaint. Instead, he expressed his delight with our event and its focus. He then handed me an envelope that contained a cash donation for the summer camp. In all, the Lord raised a total of $3,500 that night through our high-class guests. In such ways, non-Christians have participated for many years in furthering the advance of the gospel by doing business with Little Texas. Moreover, they have enjoyed themselves immensely in the process.

Over the previous two years, I had spent time traveling to different cities and searching out sites for a possible second hotel. All of my efforts had proven fruitless. It was as if the Lord was closing every door for expansion.

Late in the summer of 2003, I became convinced that the reason for this was that the Lord wanted to expand Little Texas in Iasi. Things were going extremely well with our fifteen rooms and the restaurant was a continuing success. Added to this, our conference facility was attracting a growing number of corporate clients. It was time to determine whether we could expand the number of guestrooms on our property. A geological survey revealed that we could build on the knoll at the back of our plot of land. We calculated that a sixteen-room wing would fit well into the space, as we could connect it to our existing eight-room wing. It seemed an ideal plan.

Then in September, Nelu Moraru came to me and announced that he would be leaving for three months to work with his brother in Italy. He could earn more money in a short amount of time and had already made up his mind to go. I quickly realized the impact this would have on our plans to double the size of the hotel. Without Nelu, the plans could not be carried out. It seemed that part of Nelu's reason for going was to earn enough to pay for some management courses for his wife, Maria. Maria had not gone to college and this adversely affected her self-image. So I offered to have Little Texas pay for the courses. This seemed perfectly natural, as our business would benefit from all she would learn. Nevertheless, Nelu was immovable; I could not convince him to stay.

Then it dawned on me. Nelu was now forty and had never really had any adventure in his life. He had married young, raised a family, and worked like a slave. This time in Italy was to be the extent of his mid-life crisis. Sensing this, I just smiled and wished him well. Not wanting to give in totally, I suggested that he go for just two months and then accompany me in early December to the USA to help raise funds for the new hotel wing. It was agreed.

As originally scheduled, on December 1, I flew to the South with Nelu for two intense weeks of fundraising appointments for the proposed new hotel wing at Little Texas.

The Lord opened many doors and people were extremely gracious to grant us time during their hectic schedules just ahead of the holidays. From Memphis, we drove to Birmingham for a full week of meetings, giving us time with Trevor around our schedule. We were making solid progress on our financing need for the hotel. I had prayed that the Lord would jumpstart our largest undertaking to date with $100,000 in donations from this trip. That lofty goal was now in sight. This would mean that when I put Nelu on the airplane back to Iasi on December 15, he could immediately buy all of the materials needed at the current, 2003 prices. This would avoid the price increases that we experienced at the beginning of each year. All in all, it was a wonderfully exhausting two weeks.

The year 2004 could begin with a joyous family event. After growing up together in Romania, then going off together to college in Birmingham, Alabama, Trevor and Anna McCuistion had fallen in love. They became engaged and the wedding date was set for January 3, 2004. Now they would spend the rest of their lives together.

"Saving Serghei

2004

T he year 2004 would find us embarking on the massive construction project on our Little Texas property to coincide with the spring thaw. Part of the challenge would be to build nonstop without in any way disturbing ongoing operations in the existing hotel, restaurant, and conference facilities. Not surprisingly, it was Nelu who came up with the idea of "renting" our neighbor's backyard around the corner to give us unfettered access to the back of our lot. In this manner, we were able to have thousands of bricks, tons of rebar, and a mountain of cement delivered and stacked that winter, awaiting the spring ground-breaking.

Our home-building projects were developing nicely as well. We had ended 2003 by selling the remaining three homes on the current subdivision, thus netting a tidy tithe. We were able to give $43,000 to Ecclesia, the ministry for which we originally founded the business. Gerimie Meier and Ben Onu were now plotting the start of the next six-house phase on the adjoining plot of land. Additionally, the Lord brought us other Christian investors who were attracted to the concept. This allowed our little enterprise to purchase other parcels of land around Iasi for future development as the market matured.

On the hotel-expansion front, it became necessary to seek financing from our bank in Iasi. Within the narrow window of time available, we received loan approval for $150,000 at 7.5 per cent over four years. The lender's risk was virtually zero. The reward for the Kingdom would, in the end, prove far greater.

The ministry in Moldova was continuing to bear fruit through the planting of a sister church to Taul in neighboring Tirnova. Dan Onu was traveling regularly from Iasi to these towns, and I accompanied him as my schedule allowed. The Lord's work in Moldova continued to draw me with each brief visit. The fact that many were coming to Christ through the ministry of our Romanian missionaries made investing time and money in this troubled country irresistible.

Dan's frequent trips to Moldova seemed always to result in people becoming believers, often from highly unlikely places. Dan shared with me his efforts to evangelize Serghei, the most notorious Mafia member in the Tirnova area. As an athletic, streetwise teenager, Serghei had come to the attention of the regional Mafia bosses. With zero career prospects, the lure of quick money and power made Serghei an easy target for recruitment.

Over time, Serghei became the Mafia's most feared enforcer, gaining a reputation for getting things done—anything and everything. With Mafia ties to Russia, there seemed to be an unending supply of contraband goods and all manner of illegal shenanigans in which to deal. Later, both personally and as a business, Serghei introduced drugs into the mix. This, of course, was a formula for disaster. So began Serghei's precipitous slide into the abyss. Alcohol, bloodshed, fast women, and lots of money further adorned his sinister journey. Serghei lived and took life solely at the behest of his masters. To a young man in a country whose economy had been thoroughly shredded after the fall of the Soviet Union, this seemed to be the only way out, or at least, up.

After several years of living outside the law, one of Serghei's closest comrades wanted out of the Mafia. A rumor began that Serghei, one of the Mafia leaders, took his friend into the woods, where he murdered him. Eventually, the police managed to close in and arrest Serghei. A court sentenced him to several years in prison. It was in this brutal environment, without access to drugs, that he kicked his addiction. Nearly three years later, he was back on the dirt roads of his native Tirnova. It was at about this time that Dan began reaching out to the tormented young man. Serghei began coming around to the Bible study that Dan led in Tirnova.

Not surprisingly, Serghei had more than his share of enemies and bad habits, painstakingly acquired and diligently nurtured over the lawless years. One night, after having gone on yet another alcoholic binge, he staggered back towards home and collapsed by the roadside. Sometime later, one or more ruffians came upon him and proceeded to beat the living daylights out him. After hearing the news of Serghei's condition, Dan paid a visit to his bedside. Stricken and unable to rise, Serghei tried to smile through split and swollen lips. Dan was aghast at the extent of the vicious wounds inflicted. He reasoned that such a pounding might very well have killed a lesser man.

Serghei had at last come to the end of himself. He bore all the telltale signs of having hit bottom. Gone now was the bravado, the swagger, and the arrogant sneer. Brokenness replaced the pompous façade. Dan had visited Serghei on several occasions before; he was the only one to visit him now. For this reason, Serghei was finally truly open to listen to Dan's message. Dan expressed his sorrow at the beating. He then gently, but firmly, told Serghei that there were three things that he needed to do: give up his Mafia affiliations, get a job, and accept Jesus as his Lord and Savior. Astonishingly, Serghei did all of these.

Serghei became a fixture at every church meeting. He devoured the Bible in Russian, his mother tongue. Our construction program in Tirnova needed strong workers, and Serghei needed a job; consequently, Serghei was hired as a laborer. He proved to be something of a bionic specimen. The guys slaved all day, and at night, Serghei kept the group up late, Russian Bible on his knees, plying them with surprisingly deep theological questions.

The whole town of Tirnova was abuzz with the change in Serghei. Perhaps the greatest effect was on his mother. The amazing transformation in her son so astonished her that Serghei soon led her to the Lord. This miracle somehow made the years of toil and strife in birthing Little Texas even more fulfilling.

Of course, the Lord was at work not only in Moldova, but in other places as well. Unchecked, His transforming grace was also touching many of Iasi's most disenfranchised. The 100-plus families in the Phantom apartment block had for three years been the primary target group for the ministry of the Way of Joy. Valentin and his team labored selflessly to forge trust and build bridges into the lives of dozens of families.

Here, surrogate parents had raised Nicoleta since the age of ten in a grimy and cramped room. "Mom and Dad" were engaged in the business of prostitution, right in their small room. The local police knew well about their ring of nefarious activity. If Nicoleta dared to complain, her "parents" simply threatened to put her on the street as a child prostitute. They carried out all manner of human degradation within Nicoleta's tender view for more than six years. In time, she heard about the Way of Joy center and visited more than once. Thus, Nicoleta became aware that there was a life beyond the horror of her day-to-day reality. At the Way of Joy, she was told the Good News and eventually came to faith, accepting Jesus as her Savior. Now the dilemma of desiring a new life, but seeing no means of escape from her current one, faced Nicoleta.

Distraught and desperate, she finally reached out to Valentin. She could no longer endure the life that she had known. The couple who had "cared" for her had plans to start her on a life of prostitution, as she was now sixteen. To them she was marketable flesh. However, Valentin was a man of great faith. He fervently prayed that the Lord would open a door for him to liberate Nicoleta from the nightmare she had been living. And the Lord heard those prayers.

Some years before, our clothing stores had sold donated clothing from the UK. Some of the proceeds went to help build a children's housing shelter on the southern edge of town. The director of the facility (with whom Valentin had a working relationship) quickly agreed to take Nicoleta into the home. There Nicoleta clung to her faith and grew in the Lord. Through Valentin, I was aware of Nicoleta and made sure to help with her ongoing needs through Little Texas profits. Later, Nicoleta, having turned eighteen, moved into the upper room at the Way of Joy space. Valentin shared with me her fundamental need for a sense of normalcy and for a job. In response, we hired her at Little Texas to work in the kitchen. She would show up on time for her four-hour shift, enjoy the employee meal, and then head off for her afternoon high-school-equivalency classes. Valentin gleefully related to me how Nicoleta daily returned to the WOJ bubbling over with all the news of how things had gone at "my job." In yet another example of "business as mission," Little Texas had given Nicoleta a place to which to belong, contribute, and earn her own way. Her story is that of yet another life saved; saved from a life of dehumanizing and degrading sexual slavery, and saved for eternity.

Tirnova, Moldova

October 2005

In Iasi, the intrepid Nelu and his skillful team toiled nonstop on the sixteen-room, five-story edifice. This was going on while we were again enjoying our highest-volume year ever, both in the hotel and in the restaurant. Amazingly, amid all of the new construction, we never skipped a beat in running the existing complex.

In late October 2005, I made yet another trip with Dan Onu into the Republic of Moldova. Gene Recher and Barry Coffee, two lay businessmen from Alabama, traveled with us. Our first stop, as usual, was in Tirnova. We visited with some of the town folk whom our new church plant, begun two years earlier, had begun to evangelize. As the four of us walked down a typical village dirt lane, not far from where the church met for worship, Dan recognized a man walking towards us. He was the father of a handicapped and bedridden little girl. We had come to visit them. We greeted the father, Valeriu, then followed him through the open gate of a decrepit fence, ducking to avoid badly overgrown vines.

Before we had even crossed the threshold, the pungent odor of raw, human waste instantly assaulted us. Instinctively, I sensed that the Lord had a specific purpose for us here beyond a casual visit. In an interior room, nine-year-old Valerica lay helpless in bed. The air of the room was odious, reeking of urine. Hundreds of dead insects dotted ancient strips of blackened flypaper, slung carelessly over a broken ceiling light fixture, while dozens of their kin still taunted tiny Valerica. An eclectic mix of putrid debris, festering and maggot-ridden, littered the floor.

Dan approached Valerica and began gently stroking her cheek. Her tousled brown hair was teeming with lice. Nonetheless, the child's face immediately brightened at his soft touch and warm presence. Valerica had sustained a head injury, which caused her arms and legs to be bent and crippled. She had difficulty speaking, but her mind was clear and she was very responsive. Obviously, visitors interested in her were something new.

Two other rooms, furnished like Valerica's, had dozens of empty vodka bottles strewn and discarded throughout. Beyond a doorway was a dark recess, where a rotting, fetid and grimy blanket hung. I could not even bring myself to enter. I recoiled at the overwhelming stench of human waste. Back in the entryway, I spotted a tiny wheelchair on which was piled yet another heap of moldy rubbish. Returning to the bedroom, I flashed a smile at Valerica. She was a cute little girl who seemed delighted to have company, any company.

My gaze then fixed on her father, Valeriu. My mind strained to grasp what my senses failed to comprehend. Dan informed us that Valeriu bought vodka with the small monthly stipend he received from the state for Valerica's care. Many a night, he and his cronies would booze it up right in the room where Valerica lay. Clearly, she was subsisting in deplorable conditions that many would consider inhumane even for an animal, let alone a precious little girl.

Then God seemed to make a play for my attention. The Lord revealed to me a glimpse of what He saw. I was reminded that His will for me was to no longer regard anyone from a human perspective (2 Corinthians 5:17). What I then saw in Valeriu was the disturbing image of a fallen earthly father. I saw a part of myself reflected in his face. It was all too true. Beneath this haggard, hollow-eyed façade was a beating heart and a bleeding soul. A soul that was lost just like mine before I knew Jesus. This is how the Lord had seen me. Now in that dark and desperate countenance was all that remained of that father, son, husband, and brother.

As we looked through the house, Dan found a half-buried black and white photograph. He handed it to me. It was a Polaroid picture of Valeriu and his oldest daughter, taken years earlier. Here was an attractive teenager and a proud, beaming father. I glanced from the photo to the man slouched before us on the bed. With effort, I could just recognize the man in the family photo from the now sunken, alcohol-ravaged features of Valeriu.

This family tale further unfolded through other scattered photos likewise uncovered and plucked from oblivion. The faces of grandparents, siblings, and other kin gave testimony to the family who had built their house on shifting sand in the form of Communism and its lies. Valeriu had been one of three brothers in the county's leading family during the former regime. Wealth, position, power, and influence were all theirs in abundance. Their clan had forged a small empire founded on fear, intimidation, greed, corruption, and the fiction that God did not exist.

The storms of life would soon sorely test the family's foundation. Upon hearing of his wife's rumored infidelity, Valeriu's older brother put a gun to his head and pulled the trigger. Sometime later, the youngest brother succumbed to the ravages of cancer. Later came the fall of Communism. Moldova's complete dependence on the Soviet machine caused its entire economy to implode. This family's godless worldview left them no refuge after the inevitable collapse.

The family had not heard from the older daughter, so prominent in that first photo, in years. In the blurry passage of time, Valerica was born into the abysmal family morass. At some point during this freefall, Valeriu stabbed his wife to death in a drunken rage. Now, caring strangers silently rummaged through the forlorn aftermath.

Back at Argentin's apartment, over steaming bowls of soup, we all agreed that we needed to do something for Valerica. Dan suggested we recruit Serghei, who, since giving his life to Christ, now employed his considerable strength, talent, and influence in complete submission to his Savior. Dan feared that Valeriu could turn violent upon our return. Serghei would be a dominating and persuasive presence to help spirit the father away, ostensibly on an errand to buy groceries. We arranged for an immediate and thorough scrubbing and scouring of the house. Dan would rally church volunteers.

Barry and Gene quickly rose to the task. A team of five volunteers from the church was soon hard at work on the house, inside and out. Andre, ex-rock singer-turned-worship leader, and four teenaged girls attacked the accumulated junk. Serghei's mother was also present, chattering away at Barry in Romanian, while he just nodded as if he understood every syllable.

A big part of our scheme that day was to "kidnap" Valerica. With Serghei and Valeriu now out of sight on their way to buy groceries, the moment had arrived. Jana, Argentin's wife, gingerly lifted Valerica from her wheelchair, wrapping her in an old quilt to carry her from the house to the van. She gently cradled Valerica on her lap as I drove towards their apartment in the neighboring town of Donduseni. Water was only available for a short time early in the morning and sometimes again later in the evening, so I cranked up buckets of water by hand from the well, then poured them into a large pot on the kitchen stove, to begin heating. Meanwhile, Jana played with Valerica. Each trek to the well yielded a mere two buckets, one in each hand. So back and forth I trudged and cranked until there was water enough on the stove and in the tub for a full bath.

For one solid hour, Jana bathed Valerica. The heartless neglect and physical state of this little girl shocked Jana. She said that we needed to trim her hair short as her scalp was full of parasites. Shaking with emotion, but no less focused, Jana sent me to the Russian Market to buy new clothes for Valerica. For the first time in my adult life, I took my time and had great joy in shopping for clothes. I was determined to return with exactly what Jana had instructed me to purchase.

In anticipating his time in Moldova, Gene had expressed his strong desire to actually roll up his sleeves and dig into some work project. Gene would get his wish and more. After four hours of backbreaking, odious, stomach-turning toil, the house and yard were barely recognizable: the walls were painted, the floors cleaned, the pots, pans, and utensils all scrubbed and ready for use.

Upon our return to Iasi, the Lord fast-tracked our prayer requests. Members from the church in Tirnova began daily visits to Valerica as caregivers. Her short-term living conditions demonstrably improved. This labor of love galvanized our new church plant. The whole community bore witness to this powerful testimony.

In time, our church would legally remove Valerica from her father's care and place her in a special clinic. Once there, she would begin to receive good medical care and physical therapy. Although the church continued to reach out to Valeriu, he died within a year from alcoholism. This fate was all too common for many in Moldova.

CHAPTER 37

In the Master's care

February 2006

Once Trevor, our youngest, had left Iasi to attend college, we had begun the process of adjusting to an empty nest. For Trevor, it was a happy transition to life in the USA. For Gloria, however, I sensed a subtle, but steady erosion of her joy. The blame lay in the long-term separation from our two sons and her extended family. Storm clouds steadily gathered in the emotionally charged and at times gloomy atmosphere. The clouds broke in early January 2006. We spent in-depth time sharing our struggle with caring friends. They gently, but wisely, counseled us through these uncharted waters. Our immediate game plan was to commit to no further ministry after the summer.

If the trend persisted, we faced the specter of returning home from the mission field. While we struggled with these feelings, the opportunity came for Gloria to attend a CRM women's staff retreat near Geneva in early February. I joined many others in praying for this anointed time when Gloria and thirty-four CRM women would be the objects of focused care and encouragement. At the same time, I flew to the UK to meet with the trustees of a British charity, one of our long-time partners in Iasi. Although I was physically present in London to negotiate a deal, my heavy heart was in Geneva.

Five long, lonely days later, I met Gloria's return flight at the Bucharest airport. That evening over dinner, she shared all that the Lord had done in, through, and for her. First, the Lord revealed to her that she had been angry with Him for "taking away" her children. Once she crossed that illuminating threshold, the Lord lifted the crushing weight. He then revealed the depth of His great love for her. For the first time in her life, He gave Gloria a vision. It was all about roses. She saw one rose that had bloomed vibrantly, but was now wilting. Then she saw another newly budding rose, ready to burst forth, like a brilliant new day. The God who created her knew that roses spoke Gloria Rose Little's "love language."

Through this moving mental image, God had again restored Gloria's peace with Him.

Next, the Lord addressed the lingering question of our remaining in Romania. In a conference session, one of the leaders of the retreat asked the women to meditate in the solitude of their own hearts. The object was to identify the specific place where each woman felt truly safe. For Gloria, the answer came immediately. The Lord brought to mind an image of her at our little house in Iasi, seated by my side. From that moment on, all pent up resentment and angst regarding God's call to Romania ceased. Gloria had rediscovered pure contentment in the center of His will. He gently brought her out into a spacious place, leading her beside quiet waters, restoring her soul, and guiding her on the path of righteousness for His name's sake. The Lord demonstrated my bride's life transformation by restoring her sparkling smile and dazzling eyes, and by filling her with fresh vision. Together as one, we renewed our long-term commitment to ministry in Romania, wherever it would lead, whatever it would cost.

Still basking in the warm glow of the women's retreat, Gloria helped to organize a women's prayer meeting sponsored by Little Texas. Nearly forty women from various Iasi churches turned out in our conference room to pray. Gloria knew that, by sharing her recent spiritual breakthrough, she could give glory and honor to God. However, public speaking was anathema to her. She shrank back from any opportunity to be up front or in the limelight. She felt ill equipped and inadequate. But, of course, Gloria was neither. So after much prayer, in obedience to the Spirit's prompting, Gloria used the occasion to share how the Lord had ministered to her in such a profound way. This deeply encouraged many of the faithful, but flagging, sisters. In Romania, women were the last in line for renewal and refreshment from endless labor. They were all too rarely on the receiving end of emotional nourishment, let alone spiritual succor for the thirsty soul.

Commission: Business as mission

April 2006

It had begun that lazy summer day in 1995, as I teetered on the roof of the old peasant hut. The divinely inspired vision was to go far beyond a trendy "chicken, steak, and chocolate cake place." In the ensuing years, God had blessed us with a stable, growing, and increasingly profitable venture. From our humble beginning, the Lord had grown us into a multi-million-dollar enterprise. Each year we were investing hundreds of thousands of dollars in profits into various ministries. But profit alone, while welcome and needed, was not God's ultimate end game for our little motel and diner.

In His great commission compassion, the Lord intended to use Little Texas as a relational bridge. With it, He would span the vast abyss between the truth of His salvation and the lives of business and civic leaders. Not surprisingly, people saw me as being the "owner" of Little Texas and thus not as a missionary. This provided the perfect forum for evangelistic endeavors. This divine cloaking also afforded unfettered access to many Romanian captains of commerce. Despite this, the first several years after our opening, we saw a lamentable lack of such fruit from among that virtually unreached segment of society, the wealthy. As far as I knew, only Kurt Treptow had come to Christ directly through personal witness.

As with an important client file in my briefcase, I daily carried the knowledge of my higher calling. It was deeply painful to confess the degree of shame and guilt I felt in having largely failed in living a life worthy of this facet of my calling. Now in 2006, I felt the Lord leading me as never before. He wanted me to use the forum He had provided to preach boldly His gospel. In full submission, I began again to pray fervently for open doors of opportunity. In God's free-market economy, with submission comes commission.

One Saturday afternoon in April 2006, my cell phone rang as I relaxed at home with Gloria. The man on the other end identified himself simply as Dorin Potolinca. He mentioned that he was currently a guest at Little

Texas and wondered if we could meet. He was most anxious that I purchase his hotel, located in the picturesque mountains some three hours' drive from Iasi. Such spontaneous proposals are not altogether uncommon. After all, to many in the Romanian business world, I am an entrepreneur, just one more "rich American." I offhandedly held back from snapping up his offer. Nonetheless, the voice pressed on undaunted: "My wife and I have been running this hotel for four years and it is destroying our marriage." Having myself paid no small marital price to develop Little Texas, I understood this. He then blurted out, "We are on the threshold of divorce!" Suddenly focused, I responded that I would be pleased to see him at his hotel as soon as our schedule allowed.

Two weeks later, Gloria and I arrived by car at Dorin's hotel, Ploaie de Dor ("Rain of Longing"). The massive beamed chalet, nestled in the verdant mountain splendor, was in the midst of expanding from 30 to 115 rooms. Our burly, beaming host, a man in his late forties, warmly greeted us. Over mineral water and coffee, we exchanged banal pleasantries in the second-story lounge. Then Dorin took us on a walking tour of what he had accomplished and what he hoped would soon be realized at the complex. Although my hotelier's antennae were intrigued, I was already focused on a target of a different sort.

The tour completed, Gloria politely excused herself, retiring to our cramped third-floor accommodation. Dorin and I then descended to his private office for a little man-chat. Once seated, I listened to his saga of marital woes. Clearly, Dorin was someone who had spent all his man-centered daily life feeding his pride, ego, and burgeoning appetites with scant regard for tomorrow's consequences. I sensed that we were not so different from each other. However, he was working on his third marriage. It had endured six tempestuous years. His current wife, Monica, was just thirty-one. No marriage counselor, I merely pulled out my Romanian Bible. I began to share biblical truth. It was just us two "motel men," like lifelong friends, as the Lord spoke through His Word and my life. I pointed the way to Christ. Broken and desperate, through agonized tears, Dorin confessed his sin, cried out to God, and accepted Jesus as his only hope and Savior.

As a brother in the Lord, I kept in touch, making a point of meeting with

Dorin (a six-hour round trip) to disciple him in his new-found faith. Salvation had merely been an all-important first step. For the daily walk of sanctification, however, he needed the fellowship of believers. For a middle-aged babe in Christ, there was an abundance of attendant baggage that he would have to overcome. We exchanged telephone calls a couple of times per week. On one occasion, his voice was electric with enthusiasm as he shared, "Jeri, you are the sent one from God for my life." In part, through Dorin, God was answering my prayer that Little Texas would be "business as mission." As I committed to focus more on opportunities to share my faith, the Lord continued to build bridges into the lives of Romanian business leaders.

The fundamental challenge was to create natural intersections with non-believers. Through horizontal relationships, bridges could be built that transcended preconceived biases endemic in archaic religion. Friendship could instead put the spotlight on the essential, vertical Relationship. This required opportunity, effort, and time. More importantly, it took much prayer and a powerful movement of the Holy Spirit. For us in Romania, that movement, in part, came in the form of "business as mission."

The revolution brought freedom to Romania. With freedom came choices. With choices came opportunity. With opportunity, for a growing number of Romanians, came worldly success. A new, more market-savvy generation stored up mammon while building bigger "barns." Along the way, they were writing a new chapter on conspicuous consumption. Noting this long-familiar trend, Satan simply pulled out his dog-eared American playbook. After all, it had worked so well in the USA, blinding millions for decades. The evil one was employing the same cunning in Romania. While the guns of the 1989 revolution still echoed, Romanians avidly attended the American school of values by following J. R. Ewing on the Dallas television series. For many in Romania, money, wealth, and power became the ultimate religion. Tragically, though not at all surprisingly, Satan was extremely successful in sowing his dead-end theology.

Modeling Christianity in the marketplace is one of God's chosen methods to spread His truth in Romania. As with His Word, this was a double-edged sword. On the one hand, creating higher-quality standards literally made us a leader in our industry. This put Christianity in a new and more relevant light. People remarked upon the difference they experienced in doing business with us. Our God-given reputation preceded us. This opened the door to dialogue and personal relationships. On the other hand, the burgeoning profits that resulted from doing God's business God's way created essential local funding for a variety of hands-on ministries. Business itself was a bridge. Therefore, our "commission" was to be bridge-builders into the lives of people we encountered each business day.

Ben Onu was a good example of this missional model. As a young man in his twenties, Ben was for years a part of Bob McCuistion's discipleship group. Two of his brothers, Radu and Dan, were also discipled by Bob. Ben's deepening walk with the Savior led him to seek ways in which he could influence the world around him for Christ. Ben's brothers chose a vocational missionary path, but Ben felt called to start a business that would support Romanian missionaries, like his brothers, as well as provide for the needs of his family. This gave birth in September 2000 to his vision to build houses for profit. The $15,000 initial capital investment by Little Texas in this new venture would pay handsome dividends. Through the purchase of land for speculation or for building and selling homes, Bethel would realize several hundred thousand dollars for ministry. In addition, investors would reap significant returns for making Kingdom investments to see our version of business as mission become a reality.

Reflections

As we began our sixteenth year of ministry, I looked back at a myriad of lessons learned. Among them was that God wastes nothing. Not even those things that to me appeared to be a complete waste. For example, my tenure working in restaurants during college, or my seemingly misspent year in retailing at Buffum's Department Store. The Lord had made efficient use, one way or another, of everything that had happened under His sun.

The ministry in Moldova continues to thrive. Through jointly invested profits, Little Texas and Bethel provided for a tractor to be purchased. The Lord saved Necolia out of alcoholism and is now using his skill in farming to bring in a harvest in Moldova. Ben hired Necolia to head up our first Moldovan business-as-missions project, using the tractor to cultivate and plant thirty acres of crops. The harvest yielded tons of potatoes and sunflower seeds, and the work provided much-needed wages for unemployed workers. The profits helped fund local ministry. In 2009, the plan is to double the acreage under cultivation. In addition, Little Texas has provided the funds to buy a nine-acre parcel of land to plant an apple orchard. These are small but essential steps to help Moldova become more self-sufficient in funding local ministry.

With several house churches meeting in Moldova, believers have been able to introduce Jesus to a growing number of people. A dental clinic, run by Florin's wife, Kati, became a reality. New leaders emerged under the caring discipleship of Argentin and Florin. Dan Onu and his wife, Ema, went to mission school in the Philippines, readying themselves for a lifetime of service together. Upon their return, we helped send them into Moldova to head up the ministry there. Additionally, we were able to send out and sustain yet another Romanian missionary family, Marius and Adrian Giura, who left for Siberia to reach the Buriati people.

Adi Ambrosie, an ex-pro soccer star, led his sports ministry to some sixty youths and influenced the next generation for Christ through coaching soccer. Zafi Zafiris, another soccer great, served full-time with Alege Viata (Campus Crusade/Athletes in Action), sharing his faith with coaches and players around the country. The Way of Joy ministry to the poorest of the poor has grown and deepened. We inaugurated a lunch canteen, where we fed some twenty-five hungry children several times a week. We hope in the future to increase the number of children being fed.

Mircea Detesan, one of many who suffered persecution and beatings at the hands of the former regime, continued to bring enlightened guidance to the helm of a national leadership development ministry. Additionally, Mircea remained committed to training and discipling stalwart pastors in Vietnam, who face similar persecution.

In the village of Henci, near Iasi, Tinel Baciu headed up a project that ministered to orphans who had reached young adulthood. Living and working on a small farm gave these young men a sense of purpose and belonging. Agricultural projects were begun that would provide profits for the farm to be self-sustaining. This was a community work that sought to instill Christian living and working skills in those who had only known life through the grim prism of state orphanages. In all, from profits earned in Romania, we were able to help more than twenty ministries financially on an ongoing basis.

God has by no means penned the last chapter in this story. For the first time, I sense that we are correctly positioned (doing God's work God's way) to expand on our core businesses in Romania. Furthermore, we are exploring additional start-up businesses in Moldova, as much to provide jobs as to create profits for the ongoing mission work there.

Through conversion growth over the years, God entrusted to us a group of young, committed believers who needed mentoring and shepherding to realize their full potential in the Lord. We were able to ground them in the Word, and it has taken root. Now we want to give them wings to soar as high as the Lord's call on their lives takes them. They are the first Christian, post-Communist generation. To them belong the vision, the calling, and the future face of ministry in Eastern Europe and beyond. In addition, we remain committed to helping facilitate, foster, and empower the faithful in this Kingdom labor.

In this, I pray to be used of the Lord for His purposes in the years ahead. Now in my mid-fifties, I am older than most of the Romanians with whom

I co-labor. As a companion to God's faithfulness through the passage of time and trials, I have acquired a God-centered contentment in my life. The Lord has been ever steadfast; the anchor has held amid the storms of life. Ever the master craftsman, the Lord has skillfully used Romania to grind and smooth down so many of my rough edges. I am not nearly the man that I should be, for the grace shown me. However, by God's grace, I am not the man that I was when we arrived in Iasi that snowy winter's eve in January 1993.

Reflecting over all that has taken place in and through me these past two decades, I am filled with awe and wonder when I think about why the Lord would choose to make use of such a thoroughly common lump of clay such as myself. The Lord has sovereignly transformed my weakness into His workmanship. What I have learned firsthand is this: using that which is common is part of God's plan to display His majestic might. Through ordinary, average, run-of-the pew Christians, God divinely chooses to accomplish His sovereign purpose. And that is where I came in, sitting in that Orange County pew all those years ago. Until that time (and even since), much of my life had been lived too much for me and not enough for Christ. Left to my own devices and in my own power, nothing of what has been related on these pages would have come to pass.

My prayer is that, through the tale just told, other believers might be moved to seek how they can be used in His Kingdom plan, perhaps even in "business as mission."

Ceausescu's People's Palace, Bucharest

Thrift store, Iasi

Little Texas construction, 1996

Adrian and Nelu

Little Texas John Wayne room

Lenus and Nicoleta

Valentin Chirica, "Father Teresa"

Way of Joy baptism

Bethel construction project

Little Texas hotel

Lenuta and Maria

Moldova Missions Center

Dan and Ema Onu's wedding at Little Texas

Florin and Kati Trandafir

Moldovan winter

Serghei

Moldovan baptism

Valerica

CRM EMPOWERING LEADERS

CRM (Church Resource Ministries, www.crmleaders.org) is a movement committed to developing leaders to strengthen and multiply the church worldwide. Over 300 CRM missionaries live and minister in nations on every continent, coaching, mentoring and apprenticing those called to lead and serve the Christian movement in their settings. This results in the multiplication of godly leaders who have a passion for their world and who are empowered to multiply their lives and ministry. Through them, CRM stimulates movements of fresh, authentic churches, holistic in nature, so that the name of God is renowned among the nations.

About Day One:

Day One's threefold commitment:

- To be faithful to the Bible, God's inerrant, infallible Word;
- To be relevant to our modern generation;
- To be excellent in our publication standards.

I continue to be thankful for the publications of Day One. They are biblical; they have sound theology; and they are relative to the issues at hand. The material is condensed and manageable while, at the same time, being complete—a challenging balance to find. We are happy in our ministry to make use of these excellent publications.

JOHN MACARTHUR, PASTOR-TEACHER, GRACE COMMUNITY CHURCH, CALIFORNIA

It is a great encouragement to see Day One making such excellent progress. Their publications are always biblical, accessible and attractively produced, with no compromise on quality. Long may their progress continue and increase!

JOHN BLANCHARD, AUTHOR, EVANGELIST AND APOLOGIST

Visit our website for more information and to request a free catalogue of our books.

www.dayone.co.uk